NOT TWO

The Essence of Non-Duality

Timeless Wisdom of Shankara

Padma Neppalli

INDIA · SINGAPORE · MALAYSIA

Notion Press

No.8, 3rd Cross Street,
CIT Colony, Mylapore,
Chennai, Tamil Nadu – 600004

First Published by Notion Press 2021
Copyright © Padma Neppalli 2021
All Rights Reserved.

ISBN: 978-1-63745-414-5

Contents

Translator's Note

Shri Yellamraju Srinivasa Rao was born in Andhra Pradesh, India on the 15th of July 1927. He worked as a lecturer and head of the department of Telugu in several government colleges. Realizing that Advaita (Non-Duality) Vedanta is his life's mission, he retired from service voluntarily in 1982 and dedicated the rest of his life to the study and teaching of Advaita Vedanta, the Supreme Knowledge of the Self. Shri Srinivasa Rao passed away on the 19th of December 2015.

Shri Srinivasa Rao was a staunch practitioner and renowned teacher of Advaita Vedanta. He made Shri Shankara Bhagavatpada's clarion call for Advaita his own, and tirelessly explained the fundamental principles and nuances of the Advaita doctrine to his students, taught them how to study and practice Advaita, encouraged them to stay fully committed to the teaching, and challenged them to make their Advaitic understanding an everyday experience.

I have known Shri Srinivasa Rao for over fifteen years, mainly from listening to his enlightening talks, faithfully recorded by Shri Sudhakar M. I once met Guruji at his residence in Vijayawada in 2011. It was a memorable meeting that left a lasting and profound impression on me. After a few quick introductory pleasantries, Guruji turned sharply to me and, with a penetrating look in his eyes, asked, "Are you committed to the teaching and the practice?" I mumbled something inaudible in response when he raised his hand and pointed to the various items in the room, one after the other – door, table, chair, etc. – repeatedly asking the same question, "What is this?" Before I could respond, in soft tones, he instructed, "Learn to see the wood, not the door or the table. See the substance, not the form. Make it a habit to see commonality (*sAmAnyam*) in everything, not particulars (*vishEsham*)." Overwhelmed with love and awe for this Master who did not waste a single moment to reinforce the teaching, I nodded silently. As I prepared to leave and thank him for his time, Guruji got up from his chair and opened the little cupboard in his room. He picked up the three volumes of Bhagavad Gita that he had written in Telugu and gave them to me, saying, "You will find answers to all your questions in these three volumes. Read them and call me if you have any more questions." He also picked up Vedanta Paribhasha Vivarana, the document he himself had compiled that contained an alphabetical listing of Vedantic terms and definitions, and gave it to me, saying, "Keep this. It will come in useful." The Vedanta Paribhasha has been my faithful companion since, especially during the translation of *Jagadguru Mahopadesam* to English.

In the summer of 2018, Shri Sudhakar and Shri Ramesam Vemuri encouraged me to take up the task of translating Guruji's book, *Jagadguru Mahopadesam*, from Telugu to English. I initially hesitated because I was not confident that I had the required knowledge or the necessary language skills to successfully complete the project. However, driven by a desire to share the wisdom of my teacher and the sages of the past with the English-speaking seekers of the West and of Indian origin, I agreed and plunged into the project. After more than two years of effort, under the guidance of Dr. Ramesam Vemuri, I have now completed the translation of *Jagadguru Mahopadesam* from Telugu to English and present it to you in the form of this book, now titled *Not Two: The Essence of Non-Duality*.

This is an interpretive translation of the original Telugu version and not a word-to-word translation. Keeping our Western readers in mind, we made some painful but conscientious decisions to slightly drift from the narrative Telugu idiom and style of Shri Yellamraju Srinivasa Rao. We have, however, taken extreme care not to violate the doctrine. We reworded some sentences occasionally for conciseness and rearranged some paragraphs to improve the overall flow.

If any errors have crept into the translation because of this process, I offer my sincere apologies. These errors are entirely my responsibility and may not be attributed to Shri Yellamraju Srinivas Rao or his original Telugu text.

In *Jagadguru Mahopadesam*, Guruji presents an inspired and unbiased view of Shankara's philosophy. He collected the gems of Advaita from the various texts of Shankara and strung them together beautifully into six chapters. He originally wrote this book for the Telugu-speaking community, most of whom were his students with some familiarity with the basic concepts and practices of Advaita Vedanta. Since this English version is a rendering of the original Telugu text, it also assumes its readers have a reasonable level of familiarity and prior knowledge of Advaita Vedanta.

I tried to use gender-neutral pronouns where possible but occasionally was forced to use pronouns such as he or his for simplicity and convenience only. Advaita, the Knowledge of the Self, transcends all differences. I tried to define key Sanskrit/Vedantic terms consistently in the English translation, but request my readers to forgive me if the definitions are not always consistent. Sanskrit/Vedantic terms tend to change meaning depending on the context in which they are used. For instance, the term Ishwara in the original text has been used sometimes in the colloquial sense to mean the Creator and other times in the Advaitic sense to mean Consciousness.

– Padma Neppalli
Fremont, CA, USA
December 2020

Acknowledgments

I bow in gratitude to Shri Yellamraju Srinivasa Rao garu, my beloved teacher and inspiration, for providing me with an opportunity through his book, *Jagadguru Mahopadesam*, to share his profound knowledge of Advaita Vedanta with the English-speaking seekers of the world.

This translation was made possible due to the support of family and friends dedicated to Advaita Vedanta.

I thank Shri Sudhakar M for making the original Telugu text available to me and encouraging me to translate it into English. His insights into Guruji's perspective on specific topics were valuable.

I thank Dr. Ramesam Vemuri for being my coach and guide throughout the translation of *Jagadguru Mahopadesam*. Dr. Vemuri is the author of the book *Religion Demystified*. He has translated several philosophical works, such as the Yogavasishta and Yogataravali, from Telugu to English. I am grateful to Dr. Vemuri for all his help in the translation, and for his meticulous review and editing of every chapter to make sure it adhered to the original text, in meaning and spirit.

I thank my reviewers, Shri Vijay Pargaonkar, Shri Venkat Balakrishnan, and Shri Aravinda Rao Karanam, for their expert review of this book. Their valuable feedback helped me refine the concepts and terminology presented in the book.

I am grateful to the Swamis of the various Advaita organizations for making their online resources freely available. In this translation, we have attempted to trace the various quotations and allusions Guruji makes to Shri Shankara's commentaries. To this end, we have liberally used the online resources of Shri Ramakrishna Mutt, Arsha Vidya, and other Advaita institutions to locate the quotations and the translations.

I finally thank my brother Sivakumar Patibanda and my husband Prabhakar Neppalli for acting as my sounding boards and critics throughout the translation of *Jagadguru Mahopadesam*, and my daughter Vidya Spandana for designing the front and back covers of this book.

Key to Transliteration

Letters	Sound Like	Sanskrit Examples
a	o in come	*amsa*
A	a in calm	*Atma, avidyA*
i	i in gift	*asti*
I	ee in feel	*Ishwara*
u	u in full	*buddhi*
U	oo in spoon	*pUrna*
ai	ai in tail	*dvaita*
c or ch	ch in church	*cit, sancita, chAndogya*
d	soft as in French	*dama, nididhyAsa*
N	Retroflex consonant	*prANa, pramANa*
Sh	sh in shut	*anuShThAna*
t	soft as in French	*karta, nitya*
th	th in thumb	*mithya*
Th	Retroflex consonant	*anuShThAna*
jn	Hard gy in English	*jnAna*

Note: The letter "s" is added to the end of the Sanskrit terms to indicate plural. It is preceded by a hyphen (-) to avoid confusion as being part of the Sanskrit word.

Author's Preface

Shri Shankara Bhagavatpada is revered as the Jagat-Guru, the World-Teacher. It is of great pride to us that he was born in India. The exact century in which he was born is a disputed fact even today. Some think he was born before Christ, while others think he was born after Christ. It is not of particular interest to us when or where he was born. As Shankara himself would have put it, such details are only of relative interest, and there is no point in debating them. Regardless of when or where Shankara was born, we can be assured of one thing: none in human history is comparable to Shankara because of the Indisputable and Absolute Knowledge he transmitted to the world. If the conscious human being is the epitome of creation, the Knowledge of the Absolute Self is the epitome of all Knowledge.

Numerous sciences in the world have evolved over the ages driven by common sense, scientific sense, and artistic sense. Why is the science of Advaita (Non-Dual Knowledge of the Self) considered superior to all these other sciences? The reason is that the sciences of the phenomenal world are flawed in two fundamental ways: they are relative and not final. Relative knowledge of the myriad objects in the world is like an endless ocean. However hard we may try, we will never be able to learn and master all the sciences in the world.

Knowledge of one thing depends on the knowledge of another thing, and the knowledge of that other thing depends on the knowledge of yet another thing, and so on.

Relative knowledge is incomplete because it is not conclusive. It keeps changing. Whatever was researched and established as truth in the past is proved false by contemporary research and findings. Whatever is considered true today is likely to be proved false in the future as new discoveries are made about the phenomenal world. Old knowledge becomes useless as new knowledge emerges. Relative knowledge continues to change as it evolves. Hence, every science in the world, whether it is based on common sense, scientific sense, or artistic sense, is fundamentally flawed because it is not absolute and conclusive.

The one and only Knowledge that is absolute and final is Advaita. What does Advaita mean? It means "Not Two," that there is only the Self as Pure Consciousness. Since it is the Knowledge of the One, without a second, it is Indisputable and Absolute. Relativity and contradiction are products of duality, not non-duality.

Not only is Advaita Absolute, but it also transcends the desires and goals of human existence. Human beings strive for two things all their lives – Knowledge and Happiness. Sages referred to the first as *jijnAsa* (desire to know) and the second as *mumUksha* (desire for liberation). Since, according to Advaita, Consciousness alone IS without another, there is no scope of anything else to exist. The twin desires to know and be liberated dissolve effortlessly in the understanding of the Supreme Self (Consciousness). One stays fulfilled!

A teacher who can transmit such Absolute Knowledge to the world is the most eminent of all teachers. This is evident from the title "Bhagavatpada" (The Essence of the Divine) bestowed on Shankara. Like a ball of butter in his hands, Shankara effortlessly grasped the Knowledge of the Absolute. Not only did he attain the knowledge of everything that is to be known, he experientially realized it. So complete indeed was his Knowledge of the Absolute that he came to be known as a Perfect Being (*pUrNa puruSha*).

All theories formulated in the world are based on people's experiences. We claim Advaita as the highest of all teachings, but how can it be promoted as the highest teaching if it cannot be personally validated? Even if it is promoted, of what use would it be to anyone if it cannot be understood and experienced? Shankara developed the Advaita doctrine and taught it to the world based on his own direct experience. Since he shared this profound knowledge with the rest of the world, he came to be revered as the Jagat-Guru, the World-Teacher.

The Upanishads have been offering the Knowledge of Advaita even before Shankara's advent. But that Knowledge is buried deep like precious stones in a mine. It requires great effort to discover them. Even if they are discovered, they do not shine with pure non-dual knowledge. This could confuse one into thinking that the core message of the Upanishads is duality, not non-duality! Common people as well as great scholars have been confused. Not only have they misunderstood the core message of the Upanishads, but they have also misled others by writing elaborate texts and popularizing ideas that are far from the truth. As a result, the core non-dual message of the Upanishads has been lost to the world. It is into such a world that Shankara Bhagavatpada incarnated. He resolved all the apparent differences in the scripture, gathered and polished all the gems of Advaita scattered in the Upanishads, and declared Advaita as an indisputable doctrine to the world.

Not only did Shankara establish Advaita (Non-Duality) as the core message of the Upanishads (*jnAna kANda*), he also established Advaita as the ultimate message of the Vedas (*karma kANda*). He elaborated on the *jnAna kANda* (path of knowledge) in his commentaries, as well as on the rituals and methods of worship described in the *karma kANda*, even though the two appear to conflict with each other. Karma (actions) is dualistic in nature, therefore inherently opposite to *jnAna*, which is non-dual in nature. However, according to Shankara, even karma if it is performed without any desire for specific results will culminate in non-duality. Rituals and devotional activities purify the senses and cultivate a mind that is capable of grasping the Knowledge of the Self. Therefore, according to Shankara, while the Upanishads are a direct source of Knowledge of the Self, the Vedas are an indirect source. In this manner, Shankara reconciled the apparent differences in the scripture (Action vs Knowledge) and established Advaita as the common thread in the Vedas and the Upanishads (*shruti*).

By establishing Advaita as the fundamental message of the Vedas, Shankara also established Advaita as the fundamental message of the *smriti*-s, since *smriti*-s (Manu-smriti, Yagnyavalkya-smriti, etc.)

are an interpretation of the *shruti*. Since *purANa*-s (mythology) and *itihAsa*-s (history) are based on *shruti* and *smriti*, Shankara established Advaita as the ultimate message of these texts as well. In this manner, Shankara reconciled all the differences in the various types of ancient texts and firmly established Advaita as the basis of all these texts.

Shankara's efforts to establish Advaita as the ultimate truth did not stop with scripture. He brought even the everyday, common experience of individuals into the fold of Advaita.

तस्मात् अहं ब्रह्मास्मीत्येतदवसाना एव सर्वे विधयः
सर्वाणि चेतराणि प्रमाणानि।

1.1.4, Brahma Sutra Bhashya

Shankara declared that all actions (karma) and all sources of knowledge culminate in Advaita, the undivided experience of the Self as Pure Consciousness. The phrase "all sources of knowledge" includes the literary world as well as the material world with its moving and unmoving objects. The scripture (literature) is *shabda pramANa*. It provides knowledge through its text. The objects of the world are a direct source of knowledge because we cognize them directly with our senses. The ultimate goal of the moving and unmoving objects of the world is to point to the underlying reality that is Pure Consciousness. From a tiny atom to the expansive space, everything in the world is based on this underlying reality. This is the grand synthesis that Shankara arrived at.

No one, either in the past or in the present, has demonstrated such an expansive and homogenous vision as Shankara. With a narrow view of the world, founders of the various religions have developed theories to justify their narrow views. They lacked a vision that could integrate all the differences in the world. Like blind people describing an elephant, they felt and experienced parts, but failed to see the entire truth. Since the phenomenal world with all its differences presents a fragmented view of reality, Shankara offered an integrated vision of Reality that transcended all differences.

Shankara is also known as the establisher of the six religions – Shaivisam, Vaishnavisam, Shakteyam, Ganapthyam, Sauram, and Kaumaram. All these religions believed in the existence of God, but each worshiped God in a particular form and believed that the particular form they worshiped was the most powerful of all forms. Shankara dismissed this as a biased view of God. He said the six forms (religions) were a manifestation of the six attributes of the one God: intelligence, splendor, effulgence, energy, strength, and vigor. These attributes are undifferentiated in the one Divinity, but since they are perceived as separate entities, six forms and religions have emerged. For instance, the Lord Vishnu of the Vaishnavites symbolizes intelligence, Lord Shiva of the Shaivites symbolizes effulgence, and the Goddess Shakti of the Shakti worshipers symbolizes energy. With such reasoning, Shankara reconciled the differences in the various religions and established Advaita as the fundamental truth in all religions.

स च भगवान् ज्ञानैश्वर्यशक्तिबलवीर्यतेजोभिः
सदा सम्पन्नः
Ch1 - Bhagavad Gita

This was Shankara's declaration in his commentary on Bhagavad Gita.

The reasoning with which Shankara reconciled the differences and established the various religions of his time on common ground is valid even today. The six most popular religions today, besides Hinduism, are Buddhism, Jainism, Christianity, Islam, Judaism, and Zoroastrianism. These religions also represent the different aspects of the one Divinity (Consciousness) and correspond to the religions of Shankara's time. For instance, Buddhism is a sibling to Shakteyam, Jainism to Shaivism, Christianity to Kaumaram, Islam to Vaishnavism, Judaism to Ganapathyam, and Zoroastrianism to Sauram. Using Shankara's reasoning, the differences between these religions as well can be resolved.

The six philosophical systems of ancient India are Nyaya, Vaisheshika, Samkhya, Yoga, Purva Mimamsa, and Uttara Mimamsa. Nyaya-Vaisheshika philosophies are based on theory and reasoning. Using logic, they establish Atma (*jIvAtma*) and Ishwara as real. While this sounds reasonable enough, they don't stop with that. They argue that Atma and Ishwara are separate entities. They posit that the world was created (*asat kArya vAda*), that it came into existence after it was created. Since neither of these claims aligned with the Absolute Truth, Shankara redefined the core concepts of these philosophies and resolved the differences.

Shankara reconciled the differences in Yoga and Samkhya philosophies as well. Samkhya is an atheistic philosophy, while Yoga is theistic. Both philosophies posit that the world was not created and that it existed in an un-manifested state before it manifested (*sat kArya vAda*). Shankara agreed that the world was not created (*sat kArya*), but he did not agree that the world existed in an un-manifested form before it manifested. He also did not agree with their notions of *prakriti* (nature) and *puruSha* (spirit), and the idea of a fully independent *prakriti*, so he methodically refuted these notions.

Shankara systematically analyzed Purva Mimamsa and Uttara Mimamsa philosophies and refuted notions that conflicted with the Absolute Reality. These Mimamsa-s are texts that describe the import of the Vedas. They are divided into two sections – Purva (earlier) and Uttara (later). Both accept Vedas as the primary source of knowledge. The Purva Mimamsa promotes the notion of a *jIva*, of a separate entity with a gross body who performs actions (karma) and is reborn into this world or another to enjoy the results of the actions. Shankara accepted the notion of karma and rebirth as relative truth but refuted the notion that nothing exists apart from the *jIva*, not even Ishwara. He also refuted the notion of the Purva Mimamsa that karma alone, without knowledge, can help the *jIva* attain the ultimate goal of human existence (*purushArdham*), which is liberation from the cycle of birth and death.

Since the followers of Uttara Mimamsa consider the Upanishads as the ultimate source of knowledge, they are also known as Vedantins. Unlike the followers of Purva Mimamsa, who focus only on karma, followers of Uttara Mimamsa focus on Atma, the witnessing Self. While this brings them closer to the Advaitins, they are not pure non-dualists like the Advaitins. They are dualists (*dvaita*) and qualified non-dualists (*vishistA*dvaita) with different notions of reality. They elaborate on the differences between the *jIvAtma* (individual self) and the *paramAtma* (Universal Self), but say nothing about the similarities between the two. Additionally, they posit that the phenomenal world is real, that it was actually created, and not just an appearance. Shankara could not tolerate such notions of duality in the so-called practitioners of Vedanta, so he corrected their wrong notions as well.

Shankara had a panoramic and homogeneous view of the world. His vision is like a bee that moves from flower to flower, drinking the nectar from each flower, and transforming the nectar from the various flowers into a homogeneous sweet substance called honey. When we consume the honey, we enjoy it as a whole, and not in different flavors. Shankara's panoramic vision could dissolve all differences in the world into the one Reality. It is because of such a homogeneous vision that Shankara could synthesize the differences in scriptures (*shruti/smriti*), mythologies (*purANa*-s), and historical texts (*itihasa*-s) and reveal the common reality that is the substratum of all these differences. We are forever indebted to Shankara for the treasure of knowledge he has left behind. Not only people in India, but the entire humankind is indebted to him. It is only by drinking the ambrosia of Advaita to our heart's content and liberating ourselves from *samsAra* can we repay our debt to Shankara.

When human beings have acquired immense experiential knowledge about many things in the world, why is it important that they acquire the knowledge of Advaita, we may ask? Whatever knowledge we attain in this world and however many trips we make into space to discover other planets, we must remember one thing: all the knowledge and experience we attain is relative, not absolute. Relative knowledge, however vast it might be, cannot solve the fundamental problems we confront in life. As soon as one problem is resolved, another problem creeps in. We cannot totally eradicate all problems and lead a happy life. If it was in our power to do so, we would have done so a long time ago, considering how sophisticated we have made the world we live in. The more sophisticated we make the world, the more problems we confront. Relative knowledge, worldly sciences and arts, cannot solve these problems. If they cannot, how can we consider them as valid sources of knowledge? Sages of the past dismissed relative sciences as nescience! Striving in nescience is like tilling a rocky piece of land. It will not produce any results. Striving for the Supreme Knowledge of the Self will produce the desired result – lasting happiness.

Excelling in arts and worldly sciences, such as astrology, physics, medicine, and so on, will produce short-lived pleasures (*prEyas*). What is pleasurable is not necessarily good for us (*shrEyas*). What is really good for us produces long-lasting happiness. Shankara informs us that it is the Absolute Knowledge of the Self alone that can produce such happiness. All intellectuals and adepts in spiritual practices must eventually take refuge in this Absolute Knowledge. Failing to do so will be wasting their human life.

Since Jagat-Guru Shankara has given us this treasure of Advaita knowledge, we must grasp it and make it our experience. We can do so only by a careful study of his texts. Although he has written several texts, the most prominent of them are his commentaries on the Upanishads, Brahma Sutras, and Bhagavad Gita. These commentaries are like vast oceans. Precious gems of Advaita Vedanta are abundantly available in them. We need to dive deep and explore the ocean to find these gems.

This is not an easy task. Shankara's style is simple yet deep. Lucid yet profound. Precise yet comprehensive. There is not a single word that is redundant or lacking. Every text of his is a literary masterpiece, yet it resonates with deep feeling and expression (*bhAva*). It is not a trivial task to study and understand this packed content and sophisticated writing style. Since Shankara's works are not independent texts but commentaries on the scripture, in accord with the style of the scripture, gems of non-dual wisdom are scattered throughout his texts and not particularly organized.

Due to these challenges, even though Advaita knowledge is abundantly available in Shankara's commentaries on the scripture, people have failed to grasp it fully. Disappointed at not getting the full import of Advaita from the scriptures or the commentaries, seekers have wandered off into paths that are contrary to Advaita, while others gave up the teaching in frustration, thinking it is beyond their ability to comprehend it. Some make no effort at all to learn, thinking there is nothing to gain from the teaching, while others consider it a waste of time since the teaching contradicts their own experience of the world.

In addition to describing the doctrine of Advaita, Shankara also elaborated on the process of practicing Advaita (*sAdhana*). He did not hold back any information. He revealed all the secrets in his texts. It just needs someone to make a thorough search and gather all the nuggets of wisdom buried in his texts. No one in the past or in the current times has attempted to do so. Traditional scholars of the past have learned the scriptures but without any grasp or understanding of the core Advaita teaching. They were capable of dissecting every word grammatically and providing a word-to-word meaning of the text. They indulged in arguments and useless debates about the scripture but remained silent when it came to explaining the essential teaching and practice of Advaita. Contemporary scholars, on the other hand, use their own baseless logic and reason to understand the scripture. Instead of grasping the non-dual spirit of the scripture and adhering to its core message, they draw their own conclusions based on wrong understanding and start broadcasting their theories to the rest of the world. Instead of removing wrong notions about Advaita, these scholars continue to perpetuate wrong notions about Advaita.

I have been aware of these issues for a long time and have been concerned about the dangers they pose to the Advaita teaching. I have been possessed by a burning desire to remove this danger and offer Shankara's Advaita teaching in its pure and pristine form to at least the Telugu-speaking seekers of India. A mere desire to do something is of no use. The necessary tools must be acquired to fulfill it. Only then can the desire transform into action and produce the desired result. To this end, for several years, I have been completely absorbed in studying Shankara's commentaries. Of late, I have become more aware of the limited time I had on earth and felt a compelling desire to complete the work I set out to do before it was too late. Although I was not totally satisfied and convinced that I had acquired all the necessary knowledge, I surrendered to the Divine will and embarked on this project. The product of my efforts is now in front of you. It is the result of a careful study and deep contemplation of Shankara's wisdom as revealed in his commentaries. I am offering this to you in simple Telugu language. I take no credit for this work. It is only the grace of Shankara that made this possible. At the most, I might have elaborated on some concepts that Shankara may have only hinted at and presented those concepts from a modern perspective. Even that, I consider as his grace. It is only due to his grace that I was able to find and gather all the precious gems scattered in his texts.

I intuitively identified six basic principles as fundamental to the Advaita doctrine and arranged them into six chapters for your convenience. I did not invent the chapter titles. I simply reused the terms that Shankara himself used in his commentaries. The first of the chapters is Satyam-Mithya (Reality and Illusion), followed by VyavhArikam-ParamArthikam (Relative Reality and Absolute Reality), Vastutantra-Purushatantra (Intrinsic Nature versus Human Effort), AdhyAropa-ApavAda (Superimposition and Sublation), and Jivanmukti-Videhamukti (Liberation while living versus after death). I am confident that all the major concepts of Advaita are covered in these six chapters.

If people, young or old, read this book completely, paying careful attention to the meaning of every word and concept discussed in the book, not only will they give up wrong notions of Advaita, they will also drink the nectar of Shankara's eternal wisdom to their heart's content and attain immortality. When that happens, my readers as well as myself would have attained the goal of our human existence.

– Yellamraju Srinivasa Rao

Vijayawada, AP, India

March 2014 (In the 5th Reprint of the original Telugu book)

Reality and Illusion

A clear understanding of the basic concepts of Reality (*satya*) and Illusion (*mithya*) is essential for the study of Advaita, the doctrine of non-duality elaborated by Adi Shankara, who is revered as the World-Teacher of Advaita (Non-Duality). This understanding will help us discriminate real from unreal and vice versa. Unless we know what "Reality" is, acquiring other types of knowledge is of no use. It is therefore essential that we study these basic concepts in detail.

On close observation, we realize that the entire creation (*sRiShTi*) can be grouped into three broad categories: 1) sentient beings or "individuals" like us (*jIva-s*) 2) the insentient external world (*jagat*), 3) *Ishwara*, the source or the originator of the two. Everything in nature falls into one of these three categories only. The world is perceived as names and forms. Ishwara is just an ideal, a formless entity. The individual, who is the link between the world and Ishwara, is both form and formless.

Since time immemorial, every thoughtful person, either through direct perception and experience or through handed-down knowledge from generation to generation, contemplated on the validity or the reality of these three entities. Dualists declared that all three entities (*jīva, jagat,* and *Ishwara*) are separate, independent, and real. The qualified non-dualists (Vishista-Advaitins) declared that all three are real, but Ishwara is independent, while *jīva* and *jagat* are his attributes. The third category of people, the non-dualists, posited that only Ishwara is real (true), and *jīva* and *jagat* are unreal or illusory. We now have to determine which of these is real – *jīva, jagat,* or *Ishwara?*

The dualists (*dvaita*) do not address this question at all since they believe all three are real, while the qualified non-dualists (*vishishta-advaita*) address the question partially. The non-dualists, on the other hand, address it completely. Advaita implies "not two," One without a second. If there is only One, there is no scope for any argument. Since all contradictions are resolved in Advaita, Advaita considers *dvaita* and *vishishta-advaita* as opposing doctrines and establishes Advaita as the Absolute Truth. Therefore, Shankara considered the individual and the world as unreal, and Ishwara alone as real. (Note: The word Ishwara is used here to refer to Pure Consciousness (*brahman*), and not to a Creator.)

Although Advaita is the Absolute Truth, it is hard to grasp it because it appears to contradict our common experience. *jīva* and *jagat* appear to us as real, not as unreal. If they were unreal, we should not be experiencing them. If we are experiencing them all the time, how can we say they are unreal? For that matter, we might say that the notion of Ishwara itself is unreal because we never experience the formless Ishwara the same way as we experience *jīva* and *jagat.* In that case, why insist that Ishwara, who we do not experience, is real, while *jIva* and *jagat*, which we experience every minute of our life, are unreal?

Shankara answers this question by saying we experience only a few things with our senses. Just because we experience a thing, it is not necessarily true; and if we do not experience it, it is not necessarily false. If only what we directly experience with our senses is real, then we will have to say that the blackness that we perceive in the night sky is real. Similarly, if we declare something is unreal because we have not experienced it, then we will have to admit that the many galaxies that scientists claim to have discovered do not really exist. Hence, we cannot say decisively whether something is real or unreal based on our experience, since all our experiences are based on our sensory organs. We cannot be sure that our eyes and other sensory organs are functioning correctly. Even if they are functioning correctly, we cannot be sure that they are capable of perceiving things as they really are. Therefore, we cannot come to any decisive conclusions about things based purely on our sensory experiences. We can do so only if we have a good grasp and understanding of the intrinsic nature of things.

The role of science is to define things after a close observation of their intrinsic nature. When these observations of scientists are transformed into words, it becomes a science (scripture). Scientists do not imagine things or say things just to pass time. They analyze the attributes of things and, based on their analysis, postulate a theory. Since the theory is based on a careful analysis of all aspects of a thing, it becomes a *pramANa*, a valid means of knowledge. But most people don't have such an analytical intellect. They assume whatever they experience is real. They don't delve deep and understand the fundamental nature of things. Therefore, experience-based knowledge is not as authoritative as scientific or scripture-based knowledge. Common knowledge (based on sense-experience) of whatever kind it may be is inferior to scientific knowledge. For instance, the knowledge offered by sciences, such as medicine, astrology, physics, and chemistry, is far greater than the knowledge derived from the common experience of individuals in those fields.

Advaita is also a science. It is an ocean of knowledge accumulated over time by great visionaries (seers) of the past, such as the Sages Vashishta, Vamadeva, Vyasa, and others, who have attained the Knowledge of the Self or *brahman* (*Apta*). Revered as great benefactors of humankind, these Self-realized sages have directly experienced the Absolute Truth that lies beyond the mind and senses and manifested these truths in the form of scriptures called the Vedas. Since the scriptures are a revelation and not an intellectual accomplishment by any one individual or group of individuals, they are said to be "un-authored by any human being" (*apourusheyam*). Since they provide the ultimate and undisputed (*nischita*) Knowledge of Reality, they are also called *nigama* or conclusion. Since this Knowledge has been passed down orally from generation to generation over thousands of ages, it is called *Agama* or tradition. Since the Knowledge fell upon the ears of seekers, it came to be known as *shruti*. Since the Knowledge was heard, it came to be known as *shabda* (sound).

Hence, the entire Vedic literature reveals the truth discovered by sages in deep contemplation. Since it is not a result of intellectual effort but a direct experience of reality, the scripture is the ultimate source of knowledge. Of the two parts of the Vedas, the second part called the Upanishads is superior to the earlier part called the *karma kANda*. The *karma kANda* focuses on rituals and actions, while the Upanishads focus on the Supreme Knowledge of the Self and make profound statements, such as the following about the non-dual reality:

सर्वं खल्विदं ब्रह्म — This entire world we perceive is Consciousness.

अयम् आत्मा ब्रह्म — This individual is Consciousness.

एकमेवाद्वितीयं ब्रह्म — Consciousness is the only substance in the three worlds.

There is nothing other than that. There is no individual. No world. Both are false.

Although the scripture is the source of the highest knowledge of the Self as Consciousness, it does not sever all ties with the phenomenal world. We must be able to compare and validate any assertions the scripture makes against our own common experience. Unlike relative sciences, such as physical and biological sciences, where comparisons are possible, Advaita is an absolute science. Its premise is that there is only One, and not two. It dismisses the entire world of perceptions, including the notion of an individual self, as unreal. If there is only One without another, what can we compare and validate the One against? If we cannot compare and verify for ourselves the truth, how can we say with conviction that a thing is real or unreal? Should we simply take the word of the sages who claim to have experienced the truth as evidence? But what proof do we have that these sages have actually experienced the truth, the unreality of the world?

Shankara reminds us that the scripture does not claim that the phenomenal world does not exist. The scripture says that the world will appear unreal to those who analyze the intrinsic nature of the world and recognize its appearance as illusory. For others who fail to recognize the illusory nature of the world, the world will appear real and continue to exist. For such people, there is always an opportunity to analyze the phenomenal world and verify the Absolute Truth. Shankara says Self-inquiry is the process of validating the truth. There are two parts to the enquiry: the first part is the argument or the logic (*hetu*), and the second part is the analogy (*drushtAntam*) that demonstrates the fundamental point being made by the logic. The argument supports the inferred concept; the analogy provides direct perception.

The ability to perceive and infer are both inherent in us. External instruments of knowledge, such as the eyes and other sense organs, aid in the direct perception of the truth (*pratyaksha pramANam*). Mind, the internal instrument of knowledge, helps us conceptualize the truth through inference. These are the only two means of knowledge. It is easy for us to believe anything if it can be grasped by our mind and senses. The subject that Vedanta describes is beyond the mind. That is why it is hard to grasp. If we enquire into the truth with the help of sound logic and examples, we will be able to first conceive the truth indirectly through inference and later through direct perception. We will then certainly experience the reality that the seers in the past have experienced.

Truth is not something that can be manufactured. If it can be manufactured, it cannot be truth. Sages say that they have perceived the eternal Truth. But it is their experience, not ours. If it is indeed Truth, then we should be able to experience it as well. It is only through the process of enquiry that we will be able to verify and experience the Truth. If we accept it as the Truth without enquiring and verifying for ourselves, it would be like believing there are fruit trees on the riverbank without verifying if it is a fact or a fiction. For the enquiry to be logical and productive, it must start with the scripture as the basis. If it does not do so, it would be a baseless logic that does not produce any conclusive evidence. Therefore, scripture without enquiry or enquiry without the scripture are both not useful. We must always take the truth described in the scripture as the basis and then proceed to enquire systematically. Only then, says Shankara, will we be able to verify and realize for ourselves the Absolute Truth described by the scripture.

Perhaps that is the reason why Shankara's disciples did not create new scriptures of their own. They just wrote elaborate and insightful commentaries on existing scriptures. A commentary is a form of enquiry. Such an enquiry is referred to in many ways – as a philosophy (*mImAMsA*), reflection (*mananaM*), logic (*tarkam*), application (*yukti*), and proof (*upapatti*). Shankara declared that the scripture will have an unimpeachable value only when it is verified and strengthened by evidence. Once verified, it will become a firm conviction. We will now enquire into the concepts of Reality and Illusion posited by Advaita Vedanta and establish the truth.

Of the two concepts of Reality (*satyam*) and Illusion (*mithya*), let us first understand the concept of Illusion. Once we recognize what is an illusion, we will automatically recognize what remains as Reality. This is a standard practice in Vedanta. According to traditional Vedantists, truth can be grasped only by the process of elimination – "not this, not this." This process is called enquiry. Since the falsity of the individual can be established based on the falsity of the world, the illusory nature of the world must be first understood.

The Illusory Nature of the Phenomenal World

What we perceive as the world comprises animate and inanimate objects having names and forms. They are made up of the five insentient elements – earth, water, fire, air, and space – therefore the world is insentient. Since it is insentient, it is not conscious of its own existence; it is not self-aware. Since it is not self-aware, it cannot exist on its own. For an object to exist, there must be a witness that knows of its existence. For the world to exist, it must be known to a Knower. An unwitnessed presence is not possible in this creation. The witness is none other than our Knowing Consciousness. The argument that the world exists even in the absence of a witness does not stand to reason. It is like saying we see an object even though we do not have eyes to see. If we don't have eyes, we cannot see any forms. If we cannot see a form, we cannot claim that it exists. Therefore, it is not possible for the insentient world to exist by itself. It can exist only as an object that is known to a sentient being (witness).

A contention may be raised here. How can we say that the world exists only when we become aware of it? Isn't it because the world actually exists that we are able to see it? We did not create the world ourselves. It existed even before we were born and will continue to exist after we die. Therefore, it is not rational to say that the world exists only when Consciousness perceives it.

This concept is difficult to understand. Unable to resolve this issue, philosophers across the world gave different explanations. Some said that the world alone exists, while others believed that Consciousness, which is aware of the world, only exists. The former came to be known as Materialists and the latter as Idealists. Since each of them came up with sound supporting arguments, there was no conclusive understanding. Shankara resolved this complex issue by declaring the materialistic view to be wrong and the idealistic view to be correct and provided the following supporting argument.

The world comes into existence only when it is perceived by a sentient being. It has no separate existence of its own. Only when objects come into our awareness, we become aware of their existence. One might argue that the world could exist on its own even when there is no one to perceive its existence. Who or what is it that says that the world can exist on its own? It is "I," Consciousness, that says so. If the world has an independent existence of its own, it should also have the "I AM" awareness. But it does not. It always appears as an object that is known, and never as the "knower." If neither 'I who am aware of the world' nor 'the world that is devoid of self-awareness' can vouch for its existence, then whose Existence is it that is being debated? Like an abandoned child, Existence becomes an orphan. Existence is a <u>characteristic</u>. It must belong to something. That something is Consciousness, which is aware of Existence or Beingness. Hence, the world has no independent Existence of its own, and depends on Consciousness for its existence.

When we say Consciousness, we should not confuse it with the same consciousness with which each of us perceives and experiences the world. This individual consciousness is limited. It cannot grasp the entire world completely and for the entire duration it appears. Time and space obstruct the *jIva*'s knowledge from expanding, so it is restricted. This limited knowledge does not have the capacity to transcend all limitations and become pervasive. How can such a limited knowledge or non-pervasive consciousness be a witness to this vast micro and macro-cosmic universe?

Hence, although Consciousness is the witness to the world, it is not the same as the limited consciousness of the individual. What then is this Consciousness? We said that the world must be known to Consciousness for its existence. If this Consciousness is restricted by time and space, like the individual's consciousness, it is of no use. It must transcend these limitations and expand infinitely. Unless it expands infinitely, it cannot stand as a witness to this eternal world. Seers referred to this expansive Knowledge as Ishwara or Universal Consciousness. They provisionally accepted a third entity called

Ishwara as the controller and originator of the two – the individual and the world (*jagat*). Ishwara is the eternal witness that illuminates the insentient and sentient beings that appear as the phenomenal world.

Does Consciousness also require a witness for its existence? Shankara says Consciousness does not require any witness because it is Self-aware. A witness is required only for an entity that is insentient and not self-aware. Consciousness is Awareness itself. Like a lamp does not require another lamp to illuminate it, Consciousness does not require a witness to illuminate it. If we insist that it requires one, then we will require a second witness to witness the first one. This will lead to an endless discussion with no conclusion (*anavasthA doSham*). Hence, Ishwara, the opulent Universal Consciousness, does not need a witness. Self-illumined and Self-aware, it illuminates this entire universe. The world comes alive under its illumination. Due to this inseparable relationship between *jagat* (world) and Ishwara, Shankara declared that the world does not exist independent of Ishwara (witnessing Consciousness).

There are two entities: Ishwara, the source, and *jagat,* the product. If there are two entities, the two are bound to have a cause and effect relationship with each other. Cause is that which is present from the beginning, and effect is that which emerges from the cause later. Since Ishwara is the witness, it must be present first. Therefore, Ishwara is the cause. Since the world is a manifestation of Ishwara, it is the effect. In a cause-effect relationship, Advaitists hold that the effect cannot exist separate from the cause. This is known as the *ananyathva vAda*, the doctrine of Non-Difference or Total Identity. The effect is not different from its cause. We can demonstrate this with the clay-pot example. Clay is the cause and pot is its effect. There is no pot anywhere without the clay because they both share the same Existence/Beingness (*satta*). The existence of the cause is also the existence of the effect. Beyond that, the effect does not have an independent existence of its own. Shankara says that cause-effect cannot be separated from time and space, since time and space co-arise with cause and effect. The effect extends only as far out as the cause extends and exists only for as long as the cause exists. It does not have an independent existence of its own. The pot exists only as far as the clay exists. It cannot extend even an inch beyond the limits of the clay. If it does, the form that we refer to as the pot ceases to exist. Therefore, it is the existence of the cause that ensures the existence of the effect. The effect cannot have an existence of its own, separate from the cause.

Since there cannot be two separate Existences (Beingness), there cannot be two separate entities either. For two entities to exist, they must exist separately. But in the cause-effect relationship, we see the Existence of only one thing, which is the substance (cause/clay). The other (effect) is its appearance only. If a thing exists and is visible, it is real. If it does not exist but is still visible, it is an illusion. The water in a lake is visible because it is really present. The water in the mirage appears to be overflowing, but it is only the sun rays appearing as water. Hence, the appearance of the water is not real. From this example, we understand that the effect is not different from the cause and that the cause is the real substance, and the effect is only its appearance.

If the appearance of the effect is false, why do we still see it? What we see is not the effect at all, says Shankara. It is the cause itself that appears in a particular form, which we mistake for the effect. For instance, a snake looks different when it is coiled and asleep, when it moves and slithers forward, when it spreads its hood and hisses, and when it springs forward to bite. It is the same snake that appears in four different forms in four different situations. It is not a different snake in each situation. Shankara referred to this appearance of the one substance (cause) in multiple forms as *samsthAnam* (phases). We see the various phases or aspects of the cause and give each phase a new name. But there is really nothing new. The causal substance alone Is. Everything else that we perceive is its appearance only, non-different from the substance.

Shankara offers yet another explanation to prove that the effect is non-different from the cause. We see only the qualities of the cause and nothing else in the effect. Not only Vedantins, even logicians accept this for a fact since they have theorized that the attributes of the cause prevail in the effect (*kArana gunAH kArya manu pravishanti*). Shankara says the effect cannot exist independent of the cause. Wherever we touch and feel the pot (effect), we only touch and feel the clay. If it is only the qualities of the clay that we feel everywhere, can there be a separate thing as a pot? You may say that you see a stout, round form that appears different from the clay. But the form and the name are only notional. In reality, there is only clay. There are no other qualities present in the pot other than those of the clay. Even if we perceive other qualities, as soon as we touch and feel the pot, we realize that there is only clay and nothing else. Recognizing the intrinsic nature of the cause in the effect is called *prathyabHigna*. From the point of view of *prathyabHigna*, cause alone exists with not even a trace of the effect.

While it is easy to clearly recognize the cause in the effect (*prathyabHigna*) in the pot-clay example, it is not so easy to do so in other cause-effect examples, such as the examples of milk transforming into curds or seed growing into a tree. According to Shankara, wherever a cause and effect relationship exists, it is certainly possible to recognize the cause in the effect. The cause may not always be visible due to the distance between the various stages of evolution of the effect (*parinAma viprakarsham*) or the length of time it takes for the effect to emerge from the cause. These stages are like walls separating and distancing one from the other, thereby making it difficult for us to immediately perceive the qualities of the cause in the effect. Even though we do not see them, the qualities of the cause are present, albeit hidden in the effect. If we delve deep and analyze the effect step-by-step, we will slowly start seeing the intrinsic qualities of the cause in the effect. The point is that, in some things (effects), the cause is clearly visible; in some, it is vaguely visible; and in others, it is not visible at all. Hence, it is not that the qualities of the cause are totally absent in the effect, it is just that they are not fully visible.

If the qualities of the cause are not visible in the effect, how can we say that one is the cause and the other is its effect? We can identify the cause and the effect only if there is some similarity between the two. Because cause and effect share the same attributes, only a pot emerges from the clay and only a tree emerges from the seed. Otherwise, anything could emerge from anything, even though they do not share anything in common. But this is not what we see in the world. The pot emerges only from the clay and the tree emerges only from the seed. If the effect emerges only from the cause, then it must be already present in the cause. If it was not already present, how can it emerge all of a sudden? It must be present previously in order to appear subsequently. Presence or existence (*bhAva*) cannot come out of absence or non-existence (*abhAva*). If a pot can appear suddenly out of nothing, it could also appear out of a picture, a building, and so on. But that is not the case. The pot (effect) can only come out of the clay (cause). Because the effect is concealed in the cause, wherever we perceive the effect, we recognize the qualities of the cause. Hence, whatever we perceive as the effect is only the cause and nothing else.

In other words, the manifestation of the un-manifested forms in the cause is what we call effect. When it is un-manifested, we refer to it as the cause, and when it is manifested, we refer to it as the effect. The change or difference is only in the manifested and un-manifested phases of the causal substance, and not in the substance itself. The substance alone is real. One of its forms is subtle and the other is gross. Take the example of a large beautiful carpet with colorful patterns. If it is folded and put in a corner, we will not be aware of its special qualities. If it is unfolded and spread out evenly, we will notice every interesting detail about it. This recognition does not mean that the patterns on the carpet were created or came into existence suddenly. They were present earlier too. When the carpet was folded, the patterns were not visible (un-manifested), and when it was unfolded, they became visible (manifested). The difference, therefore, is only in the manifested and un-manifested states of the effect.

Unable to comprehend this subtle difference, some scholars argue that the effect is newly created (*Arambha vAda*), while others say that it (effect) is a transformation (*parinAma*). Shankara dismisses both these arguments as meaningless. If we accept the creation theory, we will have to agree that a substance that did not exist before got newly created. If we accept the transformation theory, we will have to agree that a substance that previously existed got replaced by a new substance. Neither of these theories is scientific because a substance that did not exist before cannot suddenly come into existence, and a substance that exists now cannot stop existing in the future. If a substance is present now, it must also be present in the past and in the future. It cannot be isolated (*niranvaya*m) or absent (*abhAva*). All philosophers accept this fundamental principle. Therefore, the effect (names and forms) is neither created (*Arambha*) nor is it the result of transformation (*parinAma*).

Shankara says, since the effect is a manifestation of the cause, its appearance is illusory. When the cause manifests itself in different forms, it is called *vivarta* (changeless change or transfiguration). In whatever form it appears, it is the cause itself appearing as such and nothing else. The form is inherent in the cause. Whatever form it manifests in, the cause continues to appear without a break. Since it is continuously present, there is nothing new that is created or transformed. It simply appears as if it is new or transformed. Vedantins refer to this as the Changeless Change (*vivarta*) and also Total Identification (*thAdAtmya*m) of the effect with the cause. Cause and effect are totally identified with each other. Therefore, the effect is not newly created. It has been present in the cause always and will not cease to exist. The effect is one hundred percent non-different from the cause.

We now need to apply this principle to the concepts of *jagat* and *Ishwara*. The *jagat-Ishwara* relationship is a cause-effect relationship, where the world is the effect, and Ishwara, the originator, is the cause. However, there is something unique about Ishwara that does not exist in the causes of the phenomenal world. In the phenomenal world, an entity might be a cause for a particular effect as well as the effect of a particular cause. For instance, wood is the cause for the table and an effect for the tree. Tree is the cause for the wood and an effect for the seed. This cause-effect continuum can go on forever. Hence, every cause is also an effect in the relative world. However, Ishwara is not such a cause. Since It is the original cause of the entire universe, It is not the effect of anything. It is a cause that is not an effect. Hence, Vedantists have described Ishwara variously as the original cause, the primordial cause, and the cause of all causes.

There is yet another interesting fact about the primordial cause, Ishwara. It includes three types of causes: Material cause, Efficient cause, and Instrumental cause. For the pot, clay is the material cause, and the potter is the efficient cause. The potting wheel, water, other aids are the instrumental causes. Only when all three causes work together in a coordinated manner will the effect (pot) emerge. In the empirical world, these three are distinct from each other. Material cause does not become the efficient cause, and the efficient cause does not become the instrumental cause. However, this is not the case with the original cause, Ishwara. Ishwara integrates all three – the material cause, the efficient cause, and instrumental cause – into Itself. This is because Ishwara is the originator (cause) of the entire universe. It is a cause that is not an effect. When there is only One, there cannot be even a hint of another. Therefore, the one Ishwara carries out the functions of all three.

Ishwara, the Universal Consciousness, is the sole cause of the manifested world. There is no need for anything else, neither materials nor instruments. The Universal Consciousness, on Its own will, molded Itself in multiple ways and appears as this sentient and insentient world. It is as though gold, on its own accord, modulated itself into multiple forms and appears as necklaces, bracelets, and other ornaments. The forests, rivers, mountains, and oceans that we perceive around us are like these ornaments. Like the ornaments that are nothing but gold, everything we perceive, from the macro to the micro level, is nothing but Consciousness. All forms are non-different from Ishwara, the Universal Consciousness.

Advaita holds that the qualities of the Cause must be visible in the Effect. Since Consciousness is the cause of this entire world, its qualities must be perceivable in the world. We might argue that we don't see any evidence of that in the empirical world, but Shankara declares that the qualities of Ishwara are very much visible in the world. Ishwara has only two qualities: Existence/Beingness (*sat*) and Knowledge/Consciousness (*cit*). Observe any object in the world, whether on earth, the moon, or elsewhere in the universe. It exists (Beingness) and its existence is known (Consciousness) to us. Besides that, there is nothing noteworthy about the objects. We may notice particulars, such as tall-short, stout-thin, red-black, and good-bad. But even those particulars must exist and be known to us. The Beingness or Existence of these objects is called *asti*, and their illumination (visibility/knowability) is called *bhAti* or Consciousness. The terms *satta-sphuratha* and *sat-chit* are synonymous with *asti-bhAti*. Existence-Consciousness are the two qualities of Ishwara. It is these two qualities (*asti-bhAti*) that dominate this entire manifest world. Therefore, the world is of the essential nature of Ishwara.

The main point to note from this discussion is that the worldly objects we perceive around us and feel inside us are non-different from Consciousness. Like a dancer who poses in multiple ways, Consciousness appears in different poses. "It is the primary cause *brahman* Itself that, like an actor, evolves into the respective products up to the last one, and thus becomes the object of all empirical dealings," says Shankara in his commentary on Brahma Sutras 2.1.1.8. A dancer or an actor plays multiple roles and acts in different ways.

The roles and actions might be many, but there is only one person performing them. From the primordial matter to the human body, it is only the Supreme Self that is donning different forms, entering into everything, and carrying out all the transactions. It is the rays of Its splendor that appear as the moving and unmoving universe. There isn't a single substance other than Consciousness to be spoken about. Therefore, Consciousness is the primordial cause that appears as the illusory phenomenal world.

The Illusory Nature of the Separate Self (*jIva*)

We have so far established that the world is a false appearance. We must now establish that the individual is also a false appearance. There is a difference between the illusory natures of the individual and the world. While Consciousness appears as though transfigured as the world, it remains unchanged in the individual. According to the scripture, Ishwara entered the body of the individual without undergoing any change. Therefore, unlike the world, the individual is Consciousness Itself. However, while the Consciousness of Ishwara is Complete and Perfect, the consciousness of the individual appears limited to the body-mind. Hence, Vedantins have attributed the *kArya-kArana* (cause-effect) relationship to the world and Ishwara, and *amsa-amsi* (part-whole) relationship to the individual and Ishwara. *amsi* is the Universal or Collective Consciousness, and *amsa* is a small part of it. Like a spark that is a part of a blazing fire or a wave that is a part of the vast ocean, the individual consciousness is a fraction of the Universal Consciousness.

Unlike the ocean and the fire that are made up of parts such as waves and sparks, Consciousness is not made up of parts. It is an undivided whole. How is it then possible for the individual to be an *amsa*, a fraction of the Indivisible Consciousness? Just as the appearance of the world that is non-different from Consciousness is false, so also is the appearance of a separate individual who is non-different from Consciousness. How can something unreal appear as though real? Shankara says this is due to wrong identification with the adjunct (*upAdhi*), which is the individualized mind-body organism. An adjunct by definition is something that appears in the middle and encroaches on a previously existing substance. The adjunct is not inherent to the substance but attracts the substance. It holds the substance in its grasp and restrains it.

This concept can be illustrated with the example of a mirror. The mirror is an *upAdhi*, an adjunct. If we look into the mirror, we see our face reflected in it. Does the face exist in the mirror? No, it does not. It exists in our head. It did not break the mirror and enter it. So, what is it that we are seeing in the mirror? It is the image of our face. The face that appears in the mirror is not different from the face outside the mirror. Like the mirror, the body-mind organism is also an *upAdhi* (adjunct). Like the face appearing in the mirror, the Indivisible Consciousness seemingly enters and illumines the body. It limits its opulence to the *upAdhi*, the body. It is this limited Consciousness that we call *jIva* or the individual. The limited consciousness is a reflection of the Absolute Consciousness. Since the reflection resembles the object reflected, the individual consciousness resembles the Absolute Consciousness.

Since an object and its reflection in the empirical world are based on forms, it is possible for them to appear in an accessory (*upAdhi*), such as the mirror. However, Consciousness is formless and all-pervasive. How can such a formless, pervasive Consciousness "enter" the body-mind organism? If it does not enter it, how can it illumine it? Since the mirror example does not illustrate the concept completely, Shankara brings forth the example of the pot-space. The space in the pot appears as though confined to the pot. Just because it appears so, we cannot say that space is limited to the pot only. Space permeates everything. It is inside the pot and outside the pot too. It is infinite-space, not just pot-space. It is the infinite and formless space itself that appears to have "entered" the pot. In truth, it never really "entered" anything. How can a formless entity "enter" a form? A formless entity is expansive, all-pervasive, and not confined to a specific form. Therefore, it is a mistake to say that space entered the pot. In fact, it is not the space that entered the pot; it is the pot that entered the space! We mistakenly attribute the action of one entity to another. This is an error on our part. The moment the pot entered the space, we perceived the space as confined to the pot only and called it the pot-space. There are no two spaces, the one inside the pot and the one outside the pot. Space is one indivisible entity. Because an adjunct, such as the pot, appeared in the middle, the indivisible space appeared as though split into two. This appearance of two is due to the appearance of the adjunct, and not due to any inherent quality of space.

Like the pot, the body-mind organism is also an adjunct. Due to past actions (karma), it suddenly appeared in space-like Infinite

Consciousness and created the illusion of dividing the Indivisible Consciousness. Like space, Consciousness is also formless. Due to its association with the body, a form appeared. The form that appeared is that of the body, and not of Consciousness. Due to ignorance, we attribute the form to Consciousness. As a result, it appears as though Consciousness is trapped inside the body. Consciousness is not trapped inside the body. Like space, Consciousness is both inside and outside the body. It is indivisible. Hence, Consciousness is not of two types, an individual (*jIva*) consciousness and a Universal Consciousness (Ishwara). If It appears as though there are two, it is only due to the illusion created by the body and not due to the inherent nature of Consciousness. Therefore, just like the pot-space, the appearance of a separate individual consciousness (*jIva*) is not real.

For as long as the *upAdhi*, body-mind organism, exists, the illusion of a separate self will persist. How can we then consider it false? This question could potentially arise because of the examples we used previously. As Shankara says, examples are useful only up to a point and must be discarded after they serve their purpose. There is a fundamental difference between the worldly objects and the body-mind organism. In the example of the pot and the space, both of these entities exist separate and independent of each other. Similarly, in the example of the mirror and the reflection, the mirror and the reflection exist separate and independent of each other. However, in the case of the body-mind organism, it is not at all different from the Consciousness in which it appears. Body-mind is not a single entity. It is made of many parts – flesh, blood, senses, life-force, mind, and ego. Scientists refer to it as the microcosm. This microcosm is part of the macrocosm, the object world we see around us. We discussed earlier the nature of the object world and established that it is non-different from Consciousness and that its appearance is unreal. If the world itself is unreal, how can the body-mind organism, which is just a collection of parts, be real? It must be unreal as well. It is made up of the same five elements that the object world is made up of. Although mind and life-force (*prANa*) appear to be somewhat different, according to scientists, they also are elemental. Mind is derived from food and life-force from water. Everything we perceive is elemental. Therefore, like the phenomenal world, the body-mind organism is also a false appearance.

If the body-mind organism is not real, then the notion of an individual (*jIva*) who identifies with it is also not real. It is on the basis of the body that the notion of a separate self (*jIva*) arises. The body and the individual are mutually dependent on each other. If the very basis of an entity is not real, then how can the entity that depends on it be real? Just like the pot that appears as though it is the basis for the space, the body also appears as though it is the basis for Consciousness. Just as the pot-space appears to exist as long as the pot exists, so also the notion of the individual exists only for as long as the body-mind organism exists. Once the organism ceases to exist, like the pot-space, the notion of the separate self also ceases to exist. The body-mind organism actually never really existed. If a thing really exists, it will not cease to exist. If it ceases to exist, it means it never really existed. When Advaitists say that the world does not exist independent of Consciousness, they don't mean it will stop existing sometime in the future. They mean that it had never ever existed separate from Consciousness. Therefore, although the body is perceived, it is not real. Because it is not real, the individual (separate self) who depends on it is also not real.

The Reality that is Consciousness

We established so far that both the world and the individual are unreal. If two out of the three entities we identified are false (world and individual), then the remaining third entity, Ishwara, must be true. Let's investigate into that.

How can one be real while the other two are false? Maybe the third one (Ishwara) is also false; how can we know for sure? Shankara says that it is not possible for all three entities to be false. There must be at least one entity that is real that can vouch for the falsity of the others. There must be a knower or knowledge to recognize that something is unreal. If all three are false, then who is there to establish their falsity? If none of the three can proclaim their falsity, then all three must be real. But we just established beyond doubt that the world and the individual are both unreal. Therefore, Ishwara, the Knower or Witness, must be real.

Shankara says that it is the very falsity of the world and the individual that establishes the reality of Ishwara. How can an entity that is unreal prove the reality of another entity? When we say something is unreal, it does not mean it is totally non-existent. If it was totally non-existent, we would not perceive it at all. Although the form we perceive is unreal, the substratum on which it appears is real.

The unreal depends on the real. A lie depends on the truth! Shankara gives the example of a mirage. Wherever it appears, the mirage depends on the sunrays. Similarly, the world and the individual are unreal, but the witnessing Consciousness (Ishwara) on which they depend for their existence is real and always present. Co-joined with Consciousness, the world (*jagat*) and the individual (*jIva*) appear. If they separate themselves from Consciousness, they cease to exist. Everything that we perceive in the universe with our senses is false. However, from the perspective of the substratum (Consciousness) on which they appear, they are real. That means, as effects, they are unreal, but as the cause, they are real. Since we established Ishwara as the primordial cause of the world, the names and forms we perceive are real as Consciousness and unreal as separate objects. Shankara reveals this subtle truth in his commentary on Chandogya Upanishad. Shankara points out that names and forms by themselves are false, but when cognized as Consciousness, the substratum on which they appear, they are real.

That is how Shankara explained *mithya,* the illusory nature of the world. Ignorant of this subtle truth that Shankara masterfully conveys, a few scholars unfairly accuse him of being a Buddhist in disguise, who dismissed the world as non-existent and promoted the philosophy of Emptiness (*sUnya vAda*). Shankara had never advocated the Emptiness philosophy of the Buddhists. In fact, he repeatedly refuted it. Therefore, it is meaningless to say that Shankara promoted *sUnya vAda.* The Emptiness philosophy posits that the world does not exist. According to Shankara, however, the world exists, only as a superimposition on Consciousness. Because it is a superimposition, we only see Existence/Beingness everywhere. From the tiny atom to the expansive space, we only perceive their Existence and not non-existence. Existence/Beingness is the intrinsic nature of the phenomenal world. All names and forms belong to It. Hence, we cannot dismiss the world as non-existing, says Shankara.

Shankara defines *mithya* (illusion) as follows. When Consciousness, the substratum of the phenomenal world, appears as names and forms, it is that "appearance" that is considered an illusion. It is an illusion because the names and forms are perceived as though they have a separate existence of their own, independent of Consciousness. As we established earlier, nothing can exist separate or independent of Consciousness. Attributing a separate existence to these apparent forms is what Shankara defines as an "illusion." It would be a lie if we said the pearl is the oyster. But we would be saying the truth if we said the pearl is a pearl. If an entity assumes a different form, that assumed form is false. The individual and the world are such false appearances, since they are only a manifestation of Consciousness. As manifestations of Consciousness, they are like beacons signaling the underlying Reality, which is Consciousness.

Sages describe these names and forms as attributes of Ishwara. An attribute describes an aspect of the original substance. The original substance is Consciousness. From the viewpoint of the empirical world, which is a manifestation of Consciousness, the world and the individual are described as attributes of Consciousness. We discussed this subject to some extent earlier, but let us review it once again to make sure we understand it thoroughly.

Let us first examine why the phenomenal world is described as an attribute of Ishwara, the Universal Consciousness. The un-seen must be inferred from the seen. We never hesitate to believe what we perceive (forms) with our senses. Since our senses cannot cognize the formless Ishwara, it is hard to believe in its existence. We can enquire into its existence only with the help of the manifest world. The world is insentient. An insentient entity cannot illumine itself. It requires a sentient entity to illumine it. That sentient entity is Ishwara or Consciousness. The world is not a single entity. It is a complex collection of multiple parts. Such a complex collection of parts does not come into existence for its own sake. It comes into existence for the sake of a simpler and whole or complete entity. Such a complete entity is Ishwara. The phenomenal world is relative. Every object depends on another for its existence. If everything in the world is dependent on something, how can anything come into existence on its own? We find ourselves asking the proverbial question – what came into existence first, the seed or the tree? For this inter-dependent world of objects to come into existence, there must be an absolute and independent substance that is already existing. Consciousness is that absolute and independent substance on which the world appears. Therefore, names and forms are pointers to the underlying Reality that is Consciousness.

We can infer the existence of Consciousness from the individual as well. We earlier established that the individual is Consciousness Itself, but that the individual consciousness is not infinite like Ishwara. Consciousness manifests in every sentient being at some level or the other. It is totally un-manifested in insentient objects, while It is fully manifested in and as Ishwara. From the finite consciousness of the individual, we can infer the Infinite Consciousness of Ishwara. A small spark of fire signals a larger fire somewhere. A drop of water signals a larger body of water somewhere. Similarly, we can infer the infinite Universal Consciousness from the finite individual consciousness. Therefore, although names and forms are unreal, they signal the underlying Reality that is Consciousness.

Is Consciousness then to be cognized only indirectly through inference, or does it have an essential nature of its own? If names and forms cease to exist, would Consciousness also cease to exist? It is through similar questioning and reasoning that we had proved earlier that the world and the individual are unreal. It is now meaningless to use the same reasoning to prove that Consciousness is dependent on objects for its existence. Consciousness is the substratum on which the individual and the world appear. Therefore, Ishwara, the Universal Consciousness, has an essential nature of Its own that is independent of the world and the individual.

What is the essential nature of Ishwara? As we discussed earlier, the essential nature of Ishwara is Pure Consciousness. Shankara describes Consciousness as *shudda-buddha-mukta*, Pure-Intelligent-Ever Free. Space is pure but lacks intelligence or knowledge. The individual is intelligent but is not infinite. He is bound to the *upAdhi*, the body-mind adjunct. That which is boundless and permeates everything is Infinite. The Upanishads and commentaries resonate with the descriptions of that Infinite Consciousness. Taittiriya Upanishad describes it as *satyam-jnAnam-anantam brahma*, Absolute Truth-

Consciousness/Knowledge-Infinity. That which does not change its essential nature is Truth. If it changes or alters, it is false. An altered form is an appearance only and is not real. The clay (cause) is the real substance, while the pot is merely its appearance. In the clay-pot example, the clay is insentient. Ishwara, the primordial cause of the phenomenal world, is not only constant (True) but is also sentient. It is Knowledge/Consciousness. Every Knowledge (Knower) must have an object to know. Every object must have a Knower to be known. For a Knower to be aware (know) of an object, the object must continue to appear to it. If there are no objects to know, how can there be a Knower? The answer to this question lies in the third attribute provided by the scripture – Infinity. If a thing is limitless or endless, it is considered to be infinite. If a thing ends when another thing begins, it is considered finite. Knowledge/Consciousness alone Is and nothing else. If it appears as though there is something else, that something else would be the individual or the world. As we said earlier, the world is the effect and Ishwara is the cause. The effect cannot be different from the cause. Therefore, the world is non-different from Ishwara, the Consciousness. Since the individual is Consciousness Itself, the individual is also non-different from Ishwara. If neither the world nor the individual is different from Ishwara, how can Ishwara cease to exist when an object ceases to exist? Hence, the scripture described Ishwara as *anantam*, Infinity.

If we study the qualities of Ishwara, we find only three: Truth-Knowledge-Infinity. If there is nothing other than these three, Ishwara cannot be defined as the Lord or the Controller. For Ishwara to be called the controller, there must be some objects that are separate from

Ishwara, such as the *jIva* and *jagat*, that it can control (*Ishithva*). We just established that the world and the individual are non-different from Ishwara. If they are non-different from Ishwara, how can we say Ishwara controls them? If Ishwara cannot control them, how can we refer to it as a Controller? Therefore, Shankara suggests we define Ishwara as *brahman* or Absolute Consciousness, and not as a Lord or Controller. Because we assumed that the individual and the world are real, we also assumed that there must be a Lord who creates and controls them. Ishwara alone IS, without another. Shankara defines *brahman* in three descriptive statements: 1) It is larger than everything (*brihatvAt brahma*). 2) It contains everything in Itself, including the expansive space (*brmhanatvAt brahma*). 3) It sublates everything into Itself without a trace (*barhanatvAt brahma*). In his commentary, Shankara writes his commentary on Brahma Sutras:

निःशेषसंसारबीजाविद्याद्यनर्थनिबर्हणात्।
1.1.1 Brahma Sutra Bhashya.

When all polarities dissolve, what remains is Absolute Knowledge. The Upanishad called it *prajAna ghanam*, Great Knowledge/ Consciousness. It is like a lump of salt. Wherever you taste the lump, you only taste salt and nothing else. Pure Consciousness alone IS.

How can we grasp such Absolute Knowledge? The attributes we mentioned earlier describe different aspects of *brahman* from the empirical viewpoint, but they are not tools (*pramANa*) or means through which we can realize *brahman* or *Pure Consciousness* experientially. An attribute can help verify and confirm the presence of a substance. It provides indirect knowledge. But a *pramANa* provides direct and experiential knowledge about it. Eyes, ears, tongue, and other sense organs are such tools that help us experience sight, sound, taste, and smell. We now have to find the tools that can help us experience our Self directly as Pure Consciousness.

Shankara says that we don't need a separate tool or means of knowledge to experience Consciousness. A tool is necessary only to experience an insentient object that is not self-aware. Absolute Knowledge is not an insentient object. It is Pure Consciousness, so it is always Self-Evident. Its very nature is Pure Knowing. That is why the Upanishad declared that Knowledge is *brahman*. Therefore, we do not need an aid to experience Consciousness. It has the capacity to know Itself. Like a lamp that does not need another lamp to illumine it, Absolute Knowledge does need another knowledge or knower to illumine It.

Since Consciousness is Self-Aware, It transcends the field of objectivity. But Consciousness is not an object of knowledge. If It is not an object, how can we experience It? If we cannot experience It, what is the use of saying Consciousness alone is real and It is our essential nature? This is the question that we now need to address. Advaita insists that there is only Consciousness and nothing else, but how can we experientially realize It?

There does not seem to be an obvious answer to this question, but Shankara has a penetrating intellect and vision that can resolve this issue as well. First, he establishes that Consciousness is the subject. It is not an object of knowledge, but the Knower of the object. Therefore, as a Subject/Knower, It exists on Its own. Next, Shankara asks, who or what says that Consciousness exists on Its own? Since there is no other entity that can vouch for Its existence, Consciousness Itself must directly assert Its own existence. Since Its very nature is Consciousness, It is Self-Aware. Since It is sentient, It is Self-Evident. Hence, Consciousness is that continuous pulsating "I Am" awareness that we experience at all times. Vedantins call this pulsating Self-Awareness as *Atma* or the Self or the Subject. However, this Self is *pratyakAtma*, the individual or inner-self that is identified with the body and pulsates as a separate self. Like the inner-self, the outer-Self or the Universal Self (*paramAtma)* is also pulsating with the "I Am" awareness. This Universal Self is *brahman* or Absolute Consciousness.

However, *Atma* is not of two types, inner and outer. If we say there are two, then one becomes an object, a "not-Self." *Atma* is a single entity. It can only be an inner-Self (*pratyakAtma*), and not an outer-Self. If it is outside and not inside me, then it would be far and separate from me. If it is far and separate from me, then how can it be me? Therefore, there is only one *Atma,* and It is the inner-Self. The pulsating "I AM" awareness that we experience is the real Self or *Atma*. What then is *paramAtma* or the Universal Self? There is really nothing like a Universal Self. All there is, is only the inner-Self. As we discussed earlier, Consciousness is Infinite and Indivisible. Because the individual Self is identified so completely with the *upAdhi*, the body-mind, it appears finite. Because it appears finite, it cannot stand as a witness to the apparent universe. We established earlier that the universe cannot exist on its own without a witness. Since the universe requires a Witness, we imagined an *Atma* (Self) that transcends the individual self and called it Ishwara or the Universal Self. The Universal Self or Consciousness will always appear to be at a distance, away from us, as long as we identify with the body-mind organism. Once we stop identifying with the body-mind organism, we will experience everything as Pure Consciousness.

Therefore, the whole confusion is caused by the *upAdhi*, the body-mind organism, and our identification with it. The body-mind organism is a collection of parts, from the sense organs to the ego. None of those parts are me. I don't see any attributes of the body-mind organism in me. The organism (parts) is changing constantly, but I remain unchanged. If I also change, I would lose my essential nature and would need to acquire another. My essential nature is the "I AM" Consciousness, and nothing else. If I lose that one thing I have, then would I exist? I would not exist anywhere! But that never happens. If you ask any individual, "Do you exist?" The answer would always be "I exist"; not "I do not exist." Even if he says he does not exist, he will not stop existing. Anything that appears suddenly, will also disappear suddenly. But Consciousness is the very nature of our Self, so it is always present. The more we try to deny its existence, the stronger its presence becomes. In fact, we must first exist before we deny our existence. If we exist, then Consciousness, which is our essential nature, must also exist. We can get rid of anything in the phenomenal world, but not our essential nature. Getting rid of it implies that Consciousness must get rid of Itself! The fire cannot burn itself. An acrobat cannot stand on his own shoulder. Similarly, *Atma* or Consciousness cannot deny Its own existence.

Since the "I AM" awareness is always present, we should be able to experience our Self as Consciousness at all times. But we don't seem to experience Consciousness in deep sleep or in a coma. In death, we seem to lose it completely! If Consciousness is our essential nature, shouldn't we experience it at all times? It appears as though we don't experience it at all times. Shankara asks, who is it that is not experiencing It? Lack of experience is the absence of experience. There needs to be a witness, a Knower, even to know that something is absent. If there is a Knower/Knowing of the absence of experience, it means there is *Atma* or Consciousness. For any experience to be absent, there needs to be a witness to its absence, just like there needs to be a witness to its presence. So, we can never say Consciousness is absent. If we say so, then it is Consciousness Itself saying so, since there is nothing other than It. Therefore, Consciousness is ever-present, never absent.

Since it is always present, we should be able to experience Consciousness always. But do we not seem to experience Consciousness always. Why? This question persists. We are always experiencing Consciousness at some level or the other. However, our experience is not Pure or Perfect. In the waking state, when all our sense organs are fully functioning, we experience Consciousness with our mind and senses. In a dream state, when all senses are dormant and the mind alone is functioning, we experience Consciousness with our mind. In deep sleep, when the senses and the mind are dormant, Consciousness also seems to be dormant, although *prANa* (life-force) is active. In death, it appears as though Consciousness completely ceases to exist, since senses, mind, life-force, and all movements stop functioning, and our relationship with the body-mind organism is completely severed.

Since we identify only with our body-mind organism throughout our life, we experience *Atma* (Self) in a limited way, and not in its full potential. If the body-mind organism is absent and there were no boundaries, the *Atma* would permeate everything. We blame the body-mind organism and say it is an obstacle that prevents us from experiencing the Absolute Self. But the scriptures say that the body and mind are like sky-flowers. They are not real. But we mistakenly perceive them to be real. All we need to do is to correct our perception. Once we correct our perception, we will realize that there are no two things, Self and not-Self. There is only one thing and that is Pure Consciousness. That Consciousness is our very nature. There is no question about whether it is inner or outer Consciousness, whether it is individual or universal. When Consciousness is the very nature of the Self, nothing can exist outside of it. Names and forms and the notion of Ishwara are all contained in it. Once we recognize that our essential nature is Consciousness, *jagat* and Ishwara lose their separateness and dissolve in our Self. Since there is no "other," we will experience our own innermost Self as Pure Consciousness, *pratyakAtma*.

Hence, as long as the *upAdhi*-s (adjuncts) exist, *jIva* and *jagat* will continue to appear as separate entities, and a need for a sentient entity to control them will persist. This entity is the notional Ishwara, the Lord/Controller. Once we realize that the individual and the world are unreal and Consciousness alone is real, then the notion of Ishwara as a separate controlling entity disappears. What remains is *brahman*, Consciousness alone. As long as we believe that *brahman* resides someplace outside our body-mind, it is called *paramAtma*, Supreme Self. Once we realize that the body-mind, like the external world, is also non-existing, all notions of a separate world, individual, and Supreme Self disappear. All names and forms dissolve into Consciousness (*brahman*), and Consciousness alone remains. Since Consciousness is ever-present, It is the Truth. It is One Infinite, Indivisible, and Homogeneous Reality. The individual who is Consciousness Itself, the world which is a false appearance, and the transactional relationships between them – all these apparent differences are due to ignorance and lack of enquiry. Once we enquire systematically into the Truth, we realize that Consciousness alone IS. If It appears as though there is something other than Consciousness, then it is a mere illusion.

Conclusion

We have now completed our enquiry into the nature of Reality and have learned to distinguish Reality from Illusion. The triad – *jIva, jagat, and Ishwara* – appear to be separate and independent of each other. They also appear to be real. This impression is based on common experience, and not based on scientific knowledge or study of the scripture. Once we analyze the nature of reality and illusion using the reasoning provided by the science of Advaita, it becomes clear that there is only Consciousness, and nothing other than Consciousness. Although the world and the individual appear as separate entities due to wrong identification and lack of proper understanding, we realize that these are only false appearances. Although we cannot cognize Consciousness with our senses, since it is our essential nature, we are always experiencing It. Infinite Consciousness alone is real. Nothing else is real, neither the individual nor the world. If we insist that the world and the individual exist, then their apparent existence is false. If we insist that they do not exist, we would be stating the Truth.

Relative and Absolute Realities

In the previous chapter, we concluded that the Absolute Infinite Consciousness alone is real, and everything else that we perceive is unreal. Based on this conclusion, strictly speaking, we should not be experiencing anything other than Consciousness. But we continue to experience our separate self and the relative world every minute. Even if we try to dismiss them as an illusion, they continue to appear to us as real, and we continue to experience them. We would be deceiving ourselves if we dismiss our own experience as unreal. We cannot dismiss the scripture either because it is a science that was developed based on extensive research into the nature of reality by ancient seers. How can we accept the two, if they are mutually contradictory? How can we reconcile these two opposing views?

Reconciling Two Realities

We find ourselves trapped between a rock and a hard place. We cannot deny our common experience nor reject the wisdom of the scripture. Shankara says, although the scripture is superior to common experience because it is more scientific, to have complete confidence in its message, we must validate the scripture and verify for ourselves the truth. Until then, scripture will only be a theory and cannot be used to dismiss common experience as irrelevant.

The Buddhist philosophy, *vijnAna-vAda* (mind-consciousness theory), postulates that the world comes into existence only due to cognition and that it does not have an inherent existence of its own. It further states that all forms are empty because they do not have an essential nature of their own and depend on the mind for their existence. It might appear as though Shankara's illusion theory is similar to the Buddhist emptiness theory, but upon closer study, we realize that they are not the same.

Shankara does not say the empirical world is empty or non-existing. He says that the world exists, but it does not exist separate from Consciousness. It exists only as Consciousness. Since we engage with the world and experience its joys and sorrows as though they are real, we need to accept its relative reality as well. We cannot dismiss it altogether. Even if we realize it is unreal, we find people around us experiencing the world as real. Therefore, Shankara says, at least for the sake of those who are experiencing the world, we must agree, provisionally at least, that the empirical world exists.

Since we cannot deny our experience with the phenomenal world, Shankara called it the Relative Truth (*vyavahArika satyam*). When we engage with the world and consider our transactions with it as real, we experience it as a relative reality. The individual and the world are two such relative realities. Even though we call them "realities," they appear to be "real" only from the perspective of our common experience, and not because they are intrinsically real. If we closely examine their intrinsic natures, we do not find a separate self or a separate world. All we find is Consciousness alone. Shankara refers to this as the Absolute Truth (*pAramArthika satyam).*

By dividing truth into relative and absolute, it might seem as though we are violating the very concept of non-duality. According to Shankara, there is no need for concern. It is a concern only if we claim that Consciousness spontaneously split Itself into two entities and is no longer a single entity. But this is not the case. We accepted two levels of reality only to accommodate common experience, but not because Consciousness actually split Itself into two. Therefore, relative reality does not contaminate Pure Consciousness in any way, just like the dark spots in space do not contaminate space in any way. The impurity is in the perception and not in space.

The individual and the world are illusory appearances. The Absolute Reality, which is Pure Consciousness, is untouched by these illusory appearances. By provisionally accepting a relative reality, Shankara was able to reconcile two opposing views. By defining the empirical world as relative reality, he gave validity to common experience, while firmly establishing the One Reality described by the scripture as the Absolute Truth.

The Appearance of the Universe

An objection may be raised here. If there is only One Reality, how did that One become many? If it had remained as a single entity, we would not be experiencing a "relative" reality. But since the One became many, perhaps the Absolute Reality is inherently flawed!

Shankara agrees there is a flaw. For instance, he says, suppose we are walking outside in the dark and see a thin, long object. We immediately conclude that it is a snake and experience fear. In reality, it is a rope and not a snake. Instead of appearing as a rope, why did the rope appear as a snake? The rope appeared as a snake because it has the same attributes as the snake, such as being thin and long. We do not mistake a square object for a snake because it does not share the attributes of a snake. Therefore, an object appears as another only because it has the same attributes as the other object. It is in the very nature of the object to appear as something else.

Consciousness also has as its inherent nature (*prakriti*) a creative power (*mAya*) or energy (*shakti).* Because of this innate creative power (*mAya*), Consciousness appears as the individual and the phenomenal world. Like the attributes of the snake that are inherent in the rope, the attributes of the individual and the world (effects) are inherent in its *mAya*-power. Therefore, Consciousness, which is complete and perfect, has the power to manifest in any form. The scripture says, *te yadantara tat brahma* – your innate nature is *brahman*, and *parasya saktirvividhaiva srUyate* – power can manifest in any form.

This infinite power and capacity to manifest that is inherent to Consciousness is fundamentally different from the limited power and capacity exhibited by worldly objects. Worldly objects, such as clay and gold, can be molded into pots and ornaments. But they are not aware of the changes they undergo. Since these objects are insentient, they have no power or capacity of their own. On the other hand, sentient beings in the world have the power and capacity to manifest, but those are limited and individually fixed. For instance, animals cannot manifest at the same level as humans. Consciousness, perceived as Ishwara (Creator) by individuals in the empirical world, is neither insentient like the inert objects nor limited like the sentient individuals and other beings. Ishwara is fully aware of His infinite power and can wield it at His will. Having full control of His *mAya*-power, Ishwara manifests countless sentient and insentient forms, sustains them, and withdraws them into Himself at His will without any external help. So splendid indeed is His *mAya*-power that it created this beautiful painting of the world with all its moving and unmoving parts!

We now find ourselves suddenly in an awkward spot – from the frying pan into the fire! In an attempt to establish the relative reality of the phenomenal world, we ended up with a Creator and put Him in a difficult situation. We said that Ishwara, using His *mAya*-power, created this world of sentient and insentient beings. This implies that Ishwara is responsible for all the flaws that we perceive in this creation. According to Sage Badarayana, there are two types of flaws in creation: disparity and inequality. No two objects in the world are similar in appearance or behavior. We see differences in the immovable and movable beings in the world. Immovable beings, such as trees and plants, have *prANa* (life-force) and consume food and water. But they cannot move or defend themselves in any way if they are in danger. There are millions of different classes of living beings, viviparous and oviparous animals, insects, birds, and so on, that can move. Within each class, there are thousands of different species, each looking and behaving very differently from the others. Their bodies are structured differently. Their tendencies are different. If this entire world was created by Ishwara, why are there so many differences?

Inequality seems to be yet another flaw in creation. Humans are better off than birds and animals, while stationary beings, such as trees and plants, are worse off than birds and animals. One cannot help the other get out of misery. It seems like Ishwara created a world of differences and subjected its living beings to pain and sorrow. Every being continuously suffers from one or more of these three miseries – physical ailments, mental anxiety, or natural calamities.

Why would Ishwara, who we defined as Consciousness, create such an unequal and unfair world? If Ishwara is also subject to likes and dislikes, how can He be Consciousness, which is pure and perfect? One wonders if Ishwara is also just another individual *(jIva)* with some extraordinary powers!

Shankara says that it is true that Ishwara manifested this world and all the suffering associated with it. However, he says, Ishwara did not manifest this world carelessly without restraint. As we stated earlier, an object appears as something else because it is in the inherent nature of the object to appear as something else. Ishwara, due to His power of *mAya,* manifests the appearance of the manifold universe and makes names and forms appear as though real. Due to misconception, the individual perceives only names and forms, and not the underlying Reality that is Consciousness. Therefore, defective perception together with the inherent power of *mAya* to appear as many are the reasons for the appearance of the phenomenal world. If even one out of the two is absent, the world will cease to appear. This subtle point must be well understood.

Let us re-examine the rope-snake example. We said that the rope appears as the snake because the rope has the same attributes as the snake. We also said that the rope may appear as a snake due to an optical error in the perceiver. If the perception was correct, even if the rope had the attributes of a snake, it would only appear as the rope. Moreover, not every person who walks in the dark will necessarily mistake the rope for a snake. Only those who suffer from an optical illusion will perceive a snake, while others will only perceive a rope. If it is only because of the tendency of the rope to appear as a snake that we perceive a snake and not the rope, then everyone should be seeing a snake only and not a rope. Hence, it is both due to the innate power of Ishwara to appear as many as well as our own ignorance of our true nature that the world appears as real.

By the above discussion, we understand that although Ishwara has the power to manifest multiple forms, He cannot do so on His own accord without the aid of *avidyA* or ignorance that we suffer from. The power of *mAya* combined with our own ignorance creates the perception of a separate world. As long as we perceive names and forms instead of the underlying Reality that is Consciousness, the world as a separate entity will continue to appear to us.

Shankara illustrates this with the example of the Indian rope-trick. The magician throws a thick rope into the air and starts climbing it. After reaching the end of the rope, the magician and all his equipment crash to the floor and break into pieces. A few minutes later, the magician gets up and stands in one piece, much to the awe of the audience. Shankara says Ishwara is like the magician, and the world is like the rope that the magician throws into the air. The multitude of beings that perceive the phenomenal world as real are like the audience who stare mesmerized at the magician's performance. Like the illusion created by the magician with his power of magic, ignorance creates the illusion of names and forms. It is both the magician's power of magic and the misapprehension of the audience that created the illusion. If any one of them is missing, the magician will not be able to create the illusion (rope-trick). Similarly, the *mAya*-power of Ishwara combined with our own ignorance creates the illusion of the world. If either ignorance or the *mAya*-power is absent, we will stop seeing the illusion of names and forms.

One might object and argue that the audience was tricked into seeing an illusion only because the magician was performing the trick. The moment the magician stops performing, the audience will stop being tricked. Similarly, because Ishwara is manifesting the world, the world is appearing. If He stops manifesting, the world will stop appearing to the individual. Additionally, only because Ishwara gave the individual the ability to perceive, the individual is able to see the world! Hence, it is Ishwara who is to be blamed for the appearance of the world! Therefore, we might argue, the rope-trick analogy does not fully explain the illusory appearance of the world.

Shankara cautions us against stretching an analogy to a point where it stops working. He says the scripture gives an example to illustrate a specific concept so that we can easily understand it. Not every aspect of the example is expected to correspond exactly to every aspect of the concept or object that is being illustrated. It is enough if just a few aspects correspond. If every aspect of an example corresponds exactly to every aspect of the concept or object that it is being compared with, then there would be no difference between the example and the object; the example would become the object itself! This would defeat the very purpose of comparison. Therefore, we should use the magician's rope-trick example only to understand that ignorance and the *mAya*-power of Ishwara are the reasons for the appearance of the phenomenal world. If we try to stretch the example to understand the reasons for ignorance, we will be stretching it too far.

If we enquire deeper into this example, we realize one incredible fact. In the magician's example, the magician is separate from the audience. Since the audience is not involved in performing the trick, the magician could exert his power and hypnotize them. But this is not the case in the relative world. Ishwara is not separate from the individual. The individual self is not different from the Universal Self. Since we have not experienced this truth yet, we continue to identify ourselves with the body-mind adjunct. Because of this misidentification, we have come to regard ourselves as a separate self and created the notion of Ishwara or a Universal Self. When all adjuncts that we are identified with, such as body and mind, dissolve, we will experience our true nature as the Universal Self. Questions about what is creation and who created it will no longer arise. Self or Consciousness alone remains, with no notions of a separate individual (*jIva*), universe (*jagat*), and creator (Ishwara). If there is none other than Pure Consciousness, who is there to question? If we ourselves are Pure Consciousness, why would any question arise? Therefore, there is no scope for a separate entity like the world to be created. When there is Consciousness alone, there is no scope for anything else. We keep asking these questions because of ignorance. When the knowledge of the Self arises, all notions of a separate *jIva, jagat,* and Ishwara disappear, and Consciousness alone remains. Therefore, it is due to the ignorance of our true nature that we imagine ourselves as individuals who suffer the pains and pleasures of the world created by Ishwara. Since the individual, world, and Ishwara are only notional, they have no separate existence of their own. Hence, according to Advaita, the world was never created. This point of view is known in Advaita as *ajAta vAda* – non-origination of the universe. If something appears even though it does not really exist, it is only an illusion. Appearances come into existence only when we perceive them. This point of view is known in Advaita as the *dRiShTi sRiShTi vAda* – universe exists because it is perceived.

Therefore, it is due to a lack of Self-Knowledge that we perceive a world that does not really exist and feel threatened by it. It is only due to *avidyA* or ignorance that we imagined a Lord/Ishwara out there somewhere who created this world with His *mAya*-power. Ishwara is not separate from the individual or the world. Therefore, the notional Ishwara is not responsible for any flaws in the creation.

The Nature of Ignorance

What is ignorance? Where does it come from? Shankara says there is no point in asking such questions while we are immersed in ignorance. In fact, he says, there is no scope for such a question to arise, since there must be Knowledge (Consciousness) in order for such a question to even arise. If there is Knowledge, then where is the question of ignorance? Trying to understand what ignorance is, is like trying to search for darkness with a torch in hand. Ignorance, like darkness, will disappear in the illumination of Knowledge, since ignorance implies a lack of Knowledge. In truth, there is no entity called ignorance. It appears as though there is ignorance only because Knowledge has receded into the background. The moment Knowledge rises to the foreground, ignorance disappears! We realize that there never was ignorance, either in the past or in the present. Therefore, it is futile trying to understand what ignorance is when there is ignorance, and equally futile trying to understand what ignorance is after Knowledge arises.

Is it then worth asking from when ignorance began? Shankara says that question is also not relevant once we establish that there is no ignorance. Ignorance has no beginning, only an end. When Knowledge arises, ignorance ends. This means ignorance was present from the time Knowledge was absent! Once Knowledge is present, ignorance will be absent. Hence, ignorance, not Knowledge, was present in the past, so it has a beginning. If we try to find the beginning of ignorance in time, we will have to go into the beginning-less past! Hence, ignorance, like Consciousness, is beginning-less. However, unlike Consciousness, which is Infinite, ignorance is finite.

Advaita philosophers refer to this beginning-less ignorance as nescience. Nescience is the reason for the appearance of a separate self and the world. Vedanta defined it as the causal body. Body does not mean just the gross body parts. Anything that covers and conceals a substance is a body or a sheath. Ignorance covers Consciousness like a shadow and limits its effulgence. Such limited Consciousness is the individual, *jIva*. Hence, the notion of a separate self or individual arises only due to ignorance of the nature of the Self. If ignorance was not operating, we would be fully aware of our own nature as Pure Consciousness. We will be experiencing our full potential as Consciousness instead of experiencing ourselves as limited individuals. This experience of a limited Consciousness is enough to prove that the notion of a separate individual arises only due to ignorance.

Like the appearance of the individual, the appearance of the world is also the result of ignorance. Ignorance has two innate qualities to it: Veiling (*AvaraNa*) and Projection *(vikShepa)*. The veiling or concealing quality creates the notion of a limited self, while the projecting quality creates the notion of an external world. Consciousness, when limited, manifests as the sentient individual, while the rest of Consciousness appears as the insentient world comprising the five elements. Due to its concealing power, ignorance conceals the underlying reality or the substratum of all appearances, that is Consciousness. Due to its projecting power, it manifests the appearance of the world and the notion of a separate self. Since ignorance is the cause of both the individual and the world, it is referred to as the causal body.

The causal body is not a passive entity. It creates a subtle body. The sentient individual develops a desire to enjoy the pleasures of the insentient world. Desire is formless, and, like ignorance, it conceals Consciousness. Hence, it is referred to as a subtle body or a sheath. The subtle body comprises two things: mind (*manas*) and life-force (*prANa*). Of the two, the life-force creates the notion of a "doer" in the individual, and the mind creates the notion of an "enjoyer." Performing actions and enjoying the results – this summarizes the life of an individual. It is because of *manas* and *prANa* that the individual continuously engages with the world. Desire propels the individual into action. Since *manas* and *prANa* symbolize the individual driven by desire, they are also referred to as the *linga sharIra*, where *linga* stands for symbol and *sharIra* for body.

The subtle body or the *linga sharIra* gives rise to a third body, the gross body that is perceived with our senses. The primary function of the body is to perform actions. As stated earlier, ignorance generates desires, and desires generate actions. Karma or action is an attempt to satisfy desires. Karma includes performing actions and enjoying the results. Although the life-force and mind give rise to the notion of a doer and an enjoyer in the individual, they need assistants to do their work. Sense organs are such assistants. Cognitive sense organs, such as sight, touch, and smell, are controlled by the mind (*manas*), while organs of actions, such as speech, movement, and prehension, are controlled by the life-force (*prANa*). Since these are formless subtle energies, they need a medium or base to operate from. The medium cannot be another subtle entity. It must be a gross medium in order for the subtle sense organs to stay put in one place and operate.

The physical body that is made up of food is such a medium. As Chandogya Upanishad stated, the body is born from food, sustained by food, and dissolves in food. Food is essentially of the nature of the Earth. Hence, everything gross is considered to be made up of the earth element. It is because of the gross body that the life-force, mind, and intellect survive and function. Desire, which is the source of the mind and life-force, creates a longing for happiness, which is a form of ignorance. The five sheaths defined by the non-dualists that conceal Consciousness correspond to the causal, subtle, and gross bodies. The sheath made of food is the gross body. Life-force, mind, and intellect make up the subtle body. The sheath of bliss, a form of ignorance, is the causal body.

With the manifestation of these three bodies, the descent of the Consciousness into this limited self (individual) is complete. If there was no ignorance, Consciousness would not have moved anywhere. There would have been no need for the infinite to become finite. When ignorance in the form of a causal body appeared, Infinite Consciousness contracted into a finite entity and succumbed to desire. Desire in the form of the subtle body hardened into the gross body and became the means for Consciousness to transact with the world. These transactions are called karma. The world is the ground on which the individual performs karma. The individual is Consciousness appearing in a subtle body. It is due to ignorance, lack of Self-Knowledge, that the Infinite Consciousness appears veiled and limited to the individual.

Ignorance is not limited to the microcosm. It operates in the macrocosm as well and manifests similar adjuncts – causal, subtle, and gross bodies – at the cosmic level. The causal body in its un-manifested state is often referred to as Ishwara. When the causal body manifests as the subtle body, it is called *hiraNyagarba*. When the subtle body manifests as the gross body, it is called *virAt*. These three cosmic bodies correspond to the three bodies of the individual – *prajnya* (the causal body experienced in deep sleep), *taijasa* (the subtle body experienced in the dream state), and *vishwa* (gross body experienced in the waking state). The cosmic adjuncts through which Ishwara manifests are pure (*sattva*), so He has full control of them and is not limited by them. But this is not the case with the adjuncts through which the individual consciousness manifests. The causal, subtle, and gross bodies of the individual are not pure; they are stained by *rajas* (restless energy) and *tamas* (dullness, inertia), so Consciousness is restricted by them. Hence, pure cosmic bodies are called heavenly or divine, while individuals are called humans and even lesser intelligent beings are called animals. All these differences are only due to the play of ignorance!

We completed a full circle and have once again come to the conclusion that ignorance is the reason for the appearance of the world and the individual. Absence of Knowledge is ignorance. Therefore, there is really no such thing as ignorance. Pure Consciousness alone IS, and It is eternally present. Everything else is only an illusion.

It appears as though it is real until we enquire into its real nature. Even ignorance will appear unreal upon enquiry. If ignorance itself is unreal, how can its offspring, the individual and the world, be real? They appear as real only as long as there is ignorance. Like the disappearance of darkness on sunrise, ignorance will disappear when Knowledge arises. With the disappearance of ignorance, all notions of a separate self and world will disappear. Everything will then appear as One Undivided Infinite Consciousness.

The Division into Two States of Reality

Hence, according to Shankara, there are two states of reality, one based on ignorance and the other based on Knowledge. By defining these two states, he resolved two conflicting notions: the notion of the One Reality promoted by the scripture, and the notion of multiplicity prompted by common experience. Relative reality validates common experience, while the Absolute Reality ratifies the scripture. The individual is freed, at least from the empirical point of view, to continue to engage with the world in accordance with his or her natural tendencies. Even though multiplicity is perceived, it is limited to the relative world. Like the mirage that dissolves into the desert upon close observation, names and forms dissolve into the Self when Knowledge of the Self arises. When all apparent differences are sublated and Pure Consciousness alone remains, scriptural pronouncements that everything is *brahman* will shine as the Absolute Truth. Hence, Advaita is like a sword with two sharp edges – Relative and Absolute realities. Such reconciliation of two conflicting concepts is possible only in Advaita, an absolute science that integrates all differences.

Common (Relative) Experience

Due to a lack of inquiry and proper understanding of Shankara's philosophy, people often mistakenly assume that they have to give up the world if they follow Shankara's teaching. Accepting the non-dual reality does not imply giving up the relative world. Since we experience the world through inference and through direct means of knowledge such as the senses, we cannot dismiss it as non-existing. Shankara accepts the existence of the empirical world provisionally. He says that we can transcend the relative reality and recognize its illusory nature with the help of a superior means of knowledge (*pramANa*). The scripture is such a superior means of knowledge. If we examine the phenomenal world closely through the lens of the scripture (Upanishads), everything that we once perceived as names and forms will present itself as Consciousness only. There will be no trace of objectivity left. We will experience only the Absolute Reality.

Until we attain such a vision of Absolute Reality, ignorance will continue to project a relative world. According to Advaita, the world continues to exist as long the individual perceives it. When the individual stops perceiving names and forms, the world will stop appearing. *"yAvattAva dabhyupgamyate" "yathA dRiShTam gRihyate"* – commented Shankara many times. As long as we mistake the snake for a rope, we only see the snake and experience all the fears associated with it. Similarly, as long as we see names and forms, the relative world will continue to appear. Once Knowledge of the Self arises, names and forms will dissolve effortlessly, and the world will no longer appear as a separate entity. Shankara says the dream world we experience in sleep illustrates this point very well. We perceive many sights and situations in our dreams and experience them as real. It never crosses our mind during the dream that they are unreal. The moment we wake up from the dream and all the dream objects disappear, we realize that the dream was just an illusion. Similarly, once we are awakened from ignorance by Self-Knowledge, the waking world will cease to appear as real. Others, who are not awakened by Self-Knowledge, will continue to experience the world and its natural flow (time-space-causation) as real. In this manner, Shankara supported the common experience of mankind without compromising on the Absolute Truth stated by the scripture.

Reconciling the Differences in the Scripture

Shankara reconciles the differences in the teachings of the scripture (Vedas) in a similar manner. In the section called *karma kANda*, the scripture describes the path of action (karma) or the path of righteousness (*dharma*), and in the section called *jnAna kANda* or the Upanishads, it describes the path of knowledge. *dharma* implies multiplicity – doer, a plan of action, execution, result, and experiencer of the result. All these differences appear in the relative reality due to ignorance (*avidyA*) or lack of Self-Knowledge. According to Shankara, as long as there is ignorance, just like the empirical world, *dharma* will also continue to exist and appear as real.

Let us now understand the path of *dharma* and its impact. The actions or karma performed with this gross body is called *dharma*. Although all actions are karma, it is only righteous actions prescribed by the scripture that are called *dharma*. Actions prohibited by the scripture are called *a-dharma* or un-righteous. Traditionally, these have come to be defined as right and wrong actions, and the results thereof as merits and demerits. Actions generate results or consequences that must be experienced at some point in the future. Hence, we cannot make light of the actions we perform now. While the action itself might come to an end, the impression it leaves behind will persist. According to the ritualists and theologians, it is these impressions from past actions that take the individual (*jīva*) to other worlds after death. According to them, even if the gross body perishes, the subtle body (mind and life-force) continues its journey. Encased in the subtle body and undetected by the human eye, the *jīva* migrates to another world, carrying with it the accumulated merits and demerits of the right and wrong actions it performed while it was embodied. Merits from right actions will result in heavenly abodes, where it enjoys pleasures, and demerits from wrong actions will result in hell, where it suffers misery. Therefore, in order to experience the results of its past actions, the *jīva* continues its journey to other worlds in the subtle body. Once it exhausts all the merits and demerits accumulated from past actions, it once again takes on a gross body and returns to earth to continue to perform karma according to its past karma and tendencies. Where and how it takes birth on earth is determined by the actions it performed in the previous births. Hence, birth is determined by karma, and karma is determined by birth. This is a vicious cycle! Even while the results of past actions are being experienced and exhausted, new results are generated by new actions. Hence, in the path of *dharma*, the cycle of birth and death will continue endlessly.

Shankara says that the path of *dharma* is not just some theory described in the scripture, but that it is also our common experience. For instance, we see only disparity and inequality in the world. We see people who perform good deeds suffer, and people who perform bad deeds prosper. There must be a reason for these differences and a reason for why we experience life the way we do. The phenomenal world is driven by cause and effect relationships. People who commit horrible deeds cannot escape from experiencing the consequences of their actions. If they can, then it certainly would be an unfair and meaningless world that we live in! Like a rock in a mad man's hand that could land anywhere, the world would be extremely random and disorganized if it were not driven by cause-effect relationships. There would be no incentive for anyone to make any effort if the results were totally random and did not correspond to the effort put in. There would be no motivation to perform the right actions prescribed by the scripture if the scripture cannot guarantee the corresponding results. Hence, the world operates on cause and effect relationships. Since all the results of all actions may not be experienced right away in this very lifetime, we need multiple lives to experience them. If the results (effect) are obvious but the cause is not obvious, we attribute the cause (action) to a previous life. If the action or cause is obvious but the result or effect is not so obvious, we anticipate the result in a future life. Hence, *dharma* drives one to act (karma), and action leads to rebirth.

By accepting rebirth, we also accept the existence and continuity of the *jīva* after death. If the *jīva* does not persist and continue after the death of the body, then who is to be born again to experience the results of the actions performed in the previous life? As stated earlier, the *jīva* is the doer. When there is a doer, there must also be an experiencer! Because of the feeling of doer-ship, the individual performs actions. Every action has a result, whether or not it is immediately visible. For instance, although sound, an attribute of space, is not always manifest, we know for a fact that it is present hidden in space. Results of past actions exist as long as there is a sense of identity and an attitude of "me" (body-mind) and "mine" (objects of the world). When such identification and attitude end, results will cease to have any effect. They fade away just as spontaneously as they were created.

By accepting that the actions of the *jīva* lead to rebirth, we are also accepting that there are other worlds to which the *jīva* migrates after death. The "world" in this context is defined as the location where the results of past actions are experienced. The location could be here on earth, in heaven, or in some other world. Since the "other" worlds are not in our direct experience, we may doubt if they really exist. Shankara says, just because our minds cannot fathom the full potential of this vast universe, we cannot dismiss the existence of other worlds. The universe is extraordinarily diverse and infinite. Its depths cannot be fathomed by our finite mind and knowledge.

A multitude of movable and immovable beings, such as plants, insects, birds, and animals, live alongside us on this planet. Plants and insects have no knowledge about us, while animals might have a little knowledge. Regardless of whether or not these beings are aware of our existence, we exist. Similarly, whether or not we are aware of their existence, there may be other worlds in this universe that are inhabited by different types of beings. Perhaps it is to such beings that our ancestors referred to as gods! Birth, death, rebirth, other worlds, results, pleasure, and pain all exist from the point of view of the relative reality. This is the essence of the path of *dharma* described in the *karma kANda* section of the Vedas.

By accepting the path of karma *(dharma)* and defining it as the relative reality, Shankara gave validity to the *karma kANda* sections of the Vedas. However, he reminds us frequently that *dharma* is only a relative reality and not Absolute Reality. Shankara says, even the path of Knowledge described in the scripture (Upanishads) is relative because all teaching happens in dualistic terms, such as teacher, student, teaching, and practice. Shankara firmly declared that all means of knowledge *(pramANa)* and all transactions occur only in ignorance *(avidyA)*. Hence, the relative world exists only as long as ignorance exists. When the Knowledge of the Self arises and ignorance ceases to exist, not only the empirical world but the scripture also becomes illusory! There will be no right or wrong actions, merits or demerits anymore. There will be no rebirth or migration to other worlds. All polarities disappear, and everything will be perceived as Pure Consciousness only. When there is Consciousness alone, there is no scope for another, either the individual (*jīva*) or the world (*jagat*). Pure Consciousness alone remains without a second.

Disparity

Absolute Reality is Pure Consciousness. Since it is ever-present, the Absolute is present even in the relative, though we do not perceive it with our senses. However, there is no scope for anything relative to be present in the Absolute. If it is present, then the Absolute is no longer pure and Absolute. Dualists, such as the ritualists and worshipers, tend to see relativity even in the Absolute because they cannot grasp its formless and attribute-less, infinite nature. They are conditioned to only see duality. They think liberation is some exotic fruit in a distant heaven that one can attain only by striving and pleasing the gods! They consider God as a separate entity, different from the Self or *Atma*. They make such divisions because they are constrained by the relative reality, that is time and space, names and forms. While entangled in these differences, they try to seek liberation. Identified with time and space, they think liberation is to be attained sometime in the future in some distant place like the heaven. Identified with names and forms, they imagine a God with a form and attributes. All these differences exist only in the relative world and not in the Absolute Reality, which is Undivided Immutable Pure Consciousness.

Therefore, people with dualistic thinking make two mistakes. Their first mistake is to think that liberation is to be attained in the future, which implies that it does not exist now. If something appears suddenly in the middle and is not present earlier, then it must have a beginning. If it has a beginning, then it also has an end. If liberation has a beginning and an end, it cannot be eternal. Their second mistake is that they consider God as a separate entity. If God and the individual are two separate entities, how can God be the Self that exists in all? He will become an object of knowledge, not the "Knower" of all objects. If it is not the "Knower," it cannot be the Supreme Self. Therefore, the Supreme Self is ever-present as the Knowing Consciousness.

Shankara says we must never forget that the Absolute is immanent in the relative. There is no object in time and space that is not touched by It. Therefore, Consciousness is inherent in the relative world and can never be absent. If Consciousness is absent in the relative world and has to be attained in some distant place, then it would be just as limited as the individual consciousness. The relative world appears only when we perceive it with our mind and senses, but Pure Consciousness is always present whether or not we perceive It. This is the Absolute Truth.

Synthesis

Although the scripture describes a relative and an Absolute Reality, two such states really do not exist. There is only One Reality and that is the Absolute Undivided Pure Consciousness. Due to ignorance, we see many in the place of the One. However, ignorance is not a real substance. It is just an optical illusion that projects imaginary forms on the Absolute Reality. Like the snake projected in a rope, the external and mental worlds are projections on Consciousness. In accordance with the tendency of the individual to perceive many in the place of the One, the scripture describes both the relative and the absolute realities, and Shankara similarly expounds on them. Hence, it is neither the goal of the scripture nor the intent of Shankara to state that such a division really exists.

Scripture is a valid means of knowledge (*pramANa*). As such, it is meant to remove ignorance by providing the right knowledge. If it does not provide the right knowledge, it is not a *pramANa*. The Upanishad instructs on Self-Knowledge, so it is said to be the highest source of knowledge. Therefore, it does not promote an illusion as reality. By describing the empirical reality in such detail, isn't the scripture actually strengthening and encouraging the notion of duality, we may ask. Shankara declares that it is only in order to negate such a notion that the scripture provisionally describes the relative reality in such detail. Its intent is not to declare that the transactional world is the Ultimate Reality, but to point out its illusory nature and warn us against getting attached to it! It instructs on the nature of the Self in order to help us get rid of the ignorance that makes us see an illusion and think it is real. When Self-Knowledge arises, all relativity disappears, and everything appears as Consciousness only.

There is yet another point to note. The empirical world is just a means, a prop, to help us recognize the underlying Absolute Reality. Hence, although the scripture describes it, we should not give the relative reality an independent existence of its own and make it our sole objective in life. A prop is required only as long as there is a goal to be achieved and is discarded once the goal is achieved. Similarly, this entire universe exists as a separate entity only to remind us of the substratum on which it appears, the underlying Absolute Reality. Once such a realization occurs, the universe loses its separate existence. This is the reason why the scripture provisionally describes the "creation" of the relative world, although such a creation never really happened. This is also the reason why Shankara accepted a relative reality, while establishing Consciousness as the Absolute Reality.

A Word of Caution

Due to a lack of proper understanding of this strategy of the scripture, aspirants and scholars alike on the path to non-duality often make mistakes. They take the means to be the end and symbols to be facts. They hold on to a mantra, a ritual, or a deity and pursue it their entire life, without making any progress toward realizing the Self. Ritualists and worshipers stop halfway through the journey before they reach the goal. For ritualists, the goal is to attain the abode of their forefathers after death. For worshipers, the goal is to attain the abode of their chosen deity. After experiencing these worlds, they both will have to return to the earth and continue to perform karma. They cannot escape rebirth. They cannot be liberated from the cycle of birth and death because they take the phenomenal world to be real and actively engage with it instead of using it as a means for recognizing the underlying Absolute Reality. In spite of the rigorous practices (sAdhana) and good deeds they perform, their progress will be limited. They will continue to be born again and again into this world. Shankara cautions them about these dangers. They should not come to a dead stop at the very first milestone they reach. They have to complete the rest of the journey. He coaxes serious practitioners of Advaita to be committed to the goal, and continue relentlessly on the journey until the goal is reached.

Shankara gives a much sterner warning to scholars who consider themselves experts on the subject of non-duality. While ritualists and worshipers make mistakes due to lack of proper investigation, Shankara says erudite scholars in Advaita make boastful claims without any experiential knowledge of the Self. If one has true Self-Knowledge, one should be seeing the One and not the many. In spite of himself being the foremost amongst the renunciates (*sanyAsa*), Shankara ridicules renunciates (*sanyAsa-s*). He says that they have only renounced their homes and families, but have not transcended the relative reality and experienced the Self. External appearances and sweet talk are not indicators of Self-Knowledge. Most often, people listen to the Advaita teaching (*shravaNa*) but do not reflect (*manana*) deeply on it. Even if they reflect on it, they do not contemplate on it relentlessly until they experience the truth. Shankara admonishes those who pretend they have realized the Self without any real experience of the Self. The reason for such pretension, Shankara says, is a rudimentary understanding of the relative reality and lack of contemplation and experience (*manana* and *nididhyAsana*). Even though we know theoretically that the relative world is unreal, until we experience the Absolute Reality as *brahman*, we must continue to enquire and meditate on the truth without a break. A disturbed mind, the result of our past actions (karma), will haunt and hinder our progress. We must, therefore, continue to perform actions prescribed by the scripture to cultivate a pure mind that does not hamper our progress. But these actions must be performed without any desire for particular results. Such desire-less actions will create a pure (*sattva*) mindset that is conducive to Self-Knowledge.

Conclusion

Although Pure Consciousness is the only Reality, It appears as many. Even though the world is unreal, it is not passive; it is a source of endless misery. Ignorance of the nature of the Self is the real cause for misery. Ignorance ends with Self-Knowledge. Self-Knowledge is the ability to see everything as Pure Consciousness. By letting go of our grasp on the empirical world, we can grasp the Absolute. In order to realize the underlying Absolute Reality, we need the support of the relative world. Until we fully experience the Absolute Reality as Pure Consciousness, we must continue to engage with the world as a means to an end, cultivate good ethics, and perform right actions. If we give up these practices too early, we will confront many hurdles that will make it much harder for us to reach our goal, which is Self-realization.

Intrinsic Nature Versus Human Effort

We concluded in the previous chapter that one can grasp the Absolute Reality only from the position of empirical reality. So long as there is an effort on our part to reach the Absolute Reality, it implies that we are still stuck at the empirical world of the triad – the individual (*jIva*), the world (*jagat*), and Ishwara. How do we transcend the triad and realize the Absolute Reality? This is the question that we will address in this chapter.

Eligible Entity

Vedantins declared unequivocally that it is the individual (*jIva*) who needs to attain Self-Knowledge and realize the Absolute Reality. Besides the individual, there are only two other entities in the field: the world (*jagat*) and Ishwara (Controller). The world is nothing but inert matter. It does not have the capacity to strive (*sAdhana*) and attain something. Ishwara is perfect, Consciousness Itself, so there is no necessity for Him to do any *sAdhana*. The individual, on the other hand, is neither totally insentient like the world of matter nor perfect like Ishwara. Although the individual (*jIva*) has consciousness, his/her consciousness is not perfect like Ishwara's. Once the *jIva's* consciousness matures into perfection, the *jIva* will shine as Ishwara. Hence, it is the individual, the *jIva*, who has both the necessity and the responsibility to "seek" perfection through an appropriate means (*sAdhana*).

It is possible that the solution is in the means (*sAdhana*) itself. But first, we must define the problem and then look for a solution (in the means). Additionally, it is the one who has the problem that must look for a solution. It is the *jIva* only who has the problem because he/she is tormented by the cycle of birth and death (*samsAra*) and searches desperately for a solution (liberation).

अनित्यमसुखं लोकम् Ch 9:33, Bhagavad Gita.

"The world is impermanent and joyless."

There is not even an iota of happiness in this world. Even if there are occasional joyous moments, they are short-lived. The very word "world" (*jagat*) in Sanskrit connotes movement (from birth to death). Since change is intrinsic to the world, change is not a problem for the world. Using His power of *mAya*, Ishwara manifests the world and keeps the wheel of *samsAra* (cycle of birth and death) turning. However, like the magician who is not affected by the magic tricks he performs, Ishwara is unaffected by His power of *mAya* and its manifestation.

Continuous change and the cycle of birth and death are a problem only to the individual (*jIva*), and not to the world (*jagat*) or Ishwara. Hence, it is the individuals who feel trapped in *samsAra* and must find a way to liberate themselves. No one else can do it for them.

Fortunately, *jIva*-s have been bestowed with the capacity to seek and find a solution to their problem. According to Shankara, such a capacity comes in two forms: motivation to free themselves and the tools necessary to help them in the process. We must recognize upfront that there is a problem and be motivated to get rid of it. Merely wishing the problem to go away is of no use.

It is only we human beings who have the desire and the tools to break the cycle of *samsAra*. No other creature on earth is similarly endowed. For example, immovable objects like rocks, soil, clay, and so on do not even have the life-force (*prANa*) in them. Plants, bushes, trees, and creepers do have life-force but lack intelligence. Birds and beasts have the life-force and some intelligence, but their intelligence is driven purely by instincts stored as impressions in their genes. They do not possess the power of discrimination. Life-force, intelligence, and power of discrimination have reached a high level of perfection in human beings. That is why the sages of the past referred to the human being as "*puruSha*."

'पुरुषे त्वेवाविस्तरामात्मा स हि प्रज्ञानेन सम्पन्नतमो विज्ञातं वदति विज्ञातं पश्यति वेद श्वस्तनं वेद लोकालोकौ मर्त्येनामतमीक्षति

Shankara's commentary on Taittiriya Upanishad II-i-1.

"It is because the Universal Consciousness has manifested in the *puruSha* that he (*jIva*) is able to have an intelligent perception of the world. He has the capacity to speak, think of the future, distinguish between good and bad, and try to achieve immortality in spite of being born in a world of mortals."

Thus did the *taittirīya* describe in many words the perfection of the human being and the lack of such perfection in the birds, beasts, and other such creatures.

'अथेतरेषां पशूनामशनायापिपासे एवाभिविज्ञानम्'

Shankara's commentary on Taittiriya Upanishad II-i-1.

"As far as other living beings are concerned, their intelligence is restricted to their bodily needs, such as hunger and thirst (eat and mate)."

Human beings, thus, are the only living beings who have the motivation to be free and have fully developed tools, such as the human body and intellect, to pursue liberation.

The Process

It is necessary to take up some activity in order to accomplish anything in this world. Nothing happens by mere wishful thinking. Hence, it is necessary to follow a process (*sAdhana*) even to attain liberation.

sAdhana is a means either to create a new object that is not available right now or to obtain an object that already exists somewhere but is currently not present with us. Creating, fetching, obtaining, etc. are all actions. For instance, if we want a house, we can build a new house and move into it. Or, if we inherit an old ancestral house, we can repair it and move into it. The first is an example of creating a new thing, and the second is an example of possessing an existing thing.

While the above is true of all *sAdhana*-s or actions performed in the relative world, Shankara says that this concept of *sAdhana* is not true in Advaita. He says that *sAdhana* in Advaita does not depend on any action. It is object-dependent, the object being the Self, which is one's own intrinsic nature. It is called "*vastutantra*" in the Advaita jargon. It refers to "a thing as it exists" i.e. the existence of an entity depends on its own intrinsic nature, and not on any external object.

In contrast, if we imagine how a particular thing exists, the existence of that thing depends on our imagination, and not on its own intrinsic nature. Dependence on something else, like the mind and intellect, for its existence is called *puruShatantra* (person-dependence or dependence on human endeavor) in Advaita. Tantra, in general, implies dependency.

We depend on our intellect (*buddhi*) to understand and grasp a thing. Therefore, *puruShatantra* is also called *buddhi tantra*. "*buddhi*" provides the sense of "agency" (doer-ship) for all the actions we perform. Without the involvement of the intellect, no organ in the body can accomplish anything. Since the intellect or *buddhi* promotes the sense of doer-ship, it is also called *kartru tantra* (doer-dependent). Whatever we do, we first think with our intellect, express it in words, and then implement it in action. All three put together constitute "*puruShatantra*."

The Self (*brahman*) that the Advaitins refer to is dependent on its own intrinsic nature, so it is *vastutantra*. It is not dependent on any doer; hence it is not *puruShatantra*.

The Self (*brahman*), the Absolute Reality, is not tainted by the world or the individual. It is Non-Dual, Infinite Consciousness. Such a substance cannot be obtained through any action since it is not dependent on any "other" thing for its existence. Since there is no scope for any doer-dependent action in Self-realization, *puruShatantra* is not an appropriate means to attain Self-realization. When the very existence of a second entity is denied, there is no opportunity to "do" any action.

Action would require a doer (*karta*), the objects involved in performing the action (*kAraka*), the doing (karma), and the result (*phala*) of performing the action. These four elements are invariably present in every action. Hence, action automatically implies a dualistic world. Action-dependent techniques are not useful for realizing the non-dual Truth. For attaining the Self, the non-dual reality, the techniques used must also be non-dual. Shankara declared doer-dependent actions as useless, since they take us in the opposite direction to our goal. It is like walking in the direction of the South Pole when our objective is to reach the North Pole!

Abrogation of Action

Unless and until we transcend duality, there is no scope for liberation. Hence, our approach must be one that negates the world. Let us now delve deeper and analyze why dualistic, action-dependent techniques are not suitable for realizing the truth.

As we stated earlier, action is essential in the relative world. Action (karma) and the cycle of births and deaths (*samsAra*) complement and reinforce each other. They arise from the same source, that is nescience (*ajnAna*), and create suffering.

न हि तमः तमसो निवर्तकं भवति॥

Shankara in his commentary on Bhagavad Gita,
Ch 4, verse 18.

Shankara says emphatically that we need light to get rid of darkness. Adding loads of darkness to existing darkness will only result in denser darkness. Likewise, the more and more obsessed we are with karma, the deeper and deeper we get into the mire of ignorance and bondage.

Karma or action comes into play in four situations:

1. Origination

2. Procurement

3. Purification and Refinement

4. Decay and Destruction

Origination refers to the production of a thing. Procurement refers to obtaining the thing that is already produced. Purification or refinement is to cleanse the thing that has been procured. Purification may be done in two ways: by removing the defects in the object or by introducing certain new qualities that were not present in the object earlier. Reformative actions in the world fall into the category of purification and refinement.

Finally, decay and destruction refer to the gradual changes in the object, which result in its break-down, disintegration, and disappearance. The above four describe the lifecycle of any substance that originates from the earth and merges back into it through a series of progressive steps.

The origin and the end define the lifespan of an object. All things, mobile or immobile, in the world must pass through these four stages. There is no escape. They are victims of progressive deterioration and change.

Let us take the example of an earthen pot. It comes into existence when a potter makes it. That is its first stage – origination. When I buy it and bring it home, it becomes "mine." This is the second stage – procurement. When I clean it and use it for storing grains or pulses, it comes into my use. That is the third stage – purification. After a period of usage, it will break and eventually merge into the earth. This is the fourth stage – decay and destruction. From a tiny atom to the vast space, from a small ant to the mighty creator Brahma, every entity in the world is subject to this inexorable change.

However, whatever may be the mighty power of this inevitable change in the relative world, it fails to affect the Self, the only reality that IS. This is because the Self is not created like the other objects in the world. Self is eternal and ever existent. It cannot be manufactured. It is the source (original cause) of everything, but not a product (effect) of any source. In other words, the Self is birth-less. It cannot be procured. Procurement implies obtaining something that is not already present. But the Self, *brahman*, is beginning-less and all-pervasive. It is space-like, existing everywhere. It is inside and outside us too. We are not different from It. So, it is meaningless to say that we need to procure It, since It is already present right here and now.

Let us now consider "refinement," the third aspect of karma or action. Refinement is out of the question in the case of Self, since Self is immanent everywhere, but completely unattached to anything. It does not have a name, nor does It have a form. It is free of the *guNa*-s (attributes). Neither an attribute nor a defect can be ascribed to It. Hence, there is no need for refining or reforming It.

Decay and destruction also do not apply to the Self. Decay connotes change. A thing composed of various components or that which is divisible into various parts can decay. The immutable and formless Self cannot change or decay. In other words, the Self is inaccessible to karma!

In view of the above discussion, how can action or karma become a means to attain the Self? Absolutely not, thunders Shankara!

Refutation of Ritualistic Worship (*upAsana*)

Some think that ritualistic worship could be a means to realize the Self. Worship, devotion, and meditation all fall into *upAsana* or worship. We have already refuted the usefulness of action in realizing the Self, but let us now delve deeper into the subject.

Although worship *(upAsana)* is action, it is unlike other types of actions. While all other actions are external to the body, *upAsana* is a mental activity, so it is done internally. Hence, it is a subtle activity, not gross like the external actions we perform. It is a continuous stream of thought modifications in the mind, like the unbroken flow of viscous oil.

One might think such subtle internal actions will help in the realization of the Self. However, Shankara emphatically declares that even such subtle mental activities are of no use in obtaining the Knowledge of *brahman*, since they are all actions. If we examine the derivation of the word "*upAsana*," it becomes clear to us that it comprises activity. "*upAsana*" is *upa* + *Asana* i.e. close by + sitting, or sitting close by. It is the act of approaching and sitting close to the objective. Approaching and sitting are actions.

While the usual actions in the physical world are performed by the gross body, *upAsana* is performed by the mind. Just because it is mental, an activity cannot stop being karma. *upAsana* involves elaborate procedures. Not only the mind, but other instruments of action are also involved in the ritual. We visualize a form in the mind, chant a mantra with our lips, carry out prescribed gestures by the movement of hands, and perform other actions in ritualistic worship. External actions are, therefore, involved in worshiping. Even meditation, which is done totally within the mind, involves action, since a form is conceived and mediated upon throughout the meditation. Clearly then *upAsana* is also action (karma).

When we imagine the form of a god or goddess in our mind, it is a creation of a form that did not exist previously in the mind. Thus, this action falls into "origination." We also try to hold on to that form tightly so that it does not slip away from our mind. This is procurement. When we begin to witness the form with all sorts of embellishments and beautifications, it is refinement. If we manage to merge our minds into the god-form, then the form will stop appearing to us. This is decay and destruction. Thus, we see all the four characteristics that we discussed earlier being present in *upAsana*, even though it is a mental process. Hence, *upAsana* or worship is no different from ritualistic actions.

However, people mistakenly give a lot of importance to *upAsana*. They hope to conceive the formless *brahman* in their mind, just as they conceive the forms of other gods, such as Indra or Varuna. All the gods have an identity and a form. They are different from us in all respects. We are the worshipers, and the god-form is the worshiped. There is scope for "conceptualization" in this process. But *brahman* cannot be conceptualized. *"brahman"* does not have any conceivable attributes like a name or a specific form. It cannot be known because It is not separate from you, the Knower. One cannot, therefore, make *brahman* an object of worship. The Upanishad refutes the method of worship in the following words:

तदेव ब्रह्म त्वं विद्धि नेदं यदिदमुपासते॥

Kena Upanishad, I-5.

May you know that alone as *brahman*. *brahman* is not this which people worship.

How is it possible to conceptualize *brahman*? Shankara asks, "Will you conceive it as it really exists, or do you expect it to take a form that conforms to your conception?"

"*brahman*" is not like the gods or goddesses that take the form that we conceive them in. *brahman* does not depend on our conceptualization. If It depends, It is not *brahman* at all. Its intrinsic nature is pure "Beingness." So, *brahman* remains the same always (formless, changeless). It is not amenable to *puruShatantra*. It is *vastutantra* because it depends on Its own intrinsic nature.

Every substance in nature has its particular characteristics. Fire is hot. Water is cool. When we think of these two elements, we do so with these characteristics in mind. We cannot conceive of fire as cold or water as heat. If water appears to be hot, it is only due to its contact with fire. Heat is not a natural characteristic of water. The nature of a substance can be understood from its intrinsic properties. We cannot imagine its nature based on our whims and fancies. If we do so, it will be a misapprehension (*bhrama*) of the substance, not proper apprehension (*prama*, knowledge). It is like a pillar that we mistake for a person in dim-lighting. It is not real. It is only an illusion. *brahman* is forever the subject, not the object. Those being its characteristics, how can *brahman* be conceptualized?

We may say that we visualize *brahman* in the form of a god or goddess, externally as an idol or internally within the cave of our heart. We may try to focus our thoughts selectively on a specific form to the exclusion of all other forms. We would only be confining and conforming *brahman* to our imagination, and not meditating on *brahman* as It really IS. If we can meditate on *brahman* as It really IS (formless, timeless, unchanging), It will no longer be *upAsana* or worship. It will be the very experience of non-dual Consciousness.

If we grok the existence of a substance "as it is," from its intrinsic qualities, it is *jnAna* or Self-Knowledge. If we visualize and attribute to it a form, it is *dhyAna* or meditation. There is a huge difference between Self-Knowledge (realization) and meditation (reflection). The first is *prama* (Reality); the second is *bhrama* (illusion).

It is best to reflect on the nature of *brahman* as It IS. If we expect *brahman* to take the form that conforms to our conception, then it wouldn't be *brahman* at all. If we cognize It the very way It exists, it is no longer worship. We cannot do both, realize *brahman* as It IS and also conform It to a specific form. That is why the *shruti* says:

नेदं यदिदमुपासते ॥

Kena Upanishad, I-5.

brahman is not this which people worship.

A contention may be raised here. Why did the scripture (*shruti*) describe *brahman,* the formless reality, and also the worship of a deity with form? The scripture did so only to accord with the spiritual capacities of the seekers, and not to promote worship as the recommended method.

In summary, just as external actions do not lead to *brahman* (Self-Knowledge), so also internal worship does not lead to *brahman*. The Self is not a substance that can be newly generated. Hence, action is of no use for its realization. Since *brahman* does not change based on the form in which we conceptualize it, worship does not help in the realization of *brahman*.

People are tired of running to different pilgrimage centers. They are exhausted with prostrating before all and sundry idols of gods and goddesses everywhere. Their energy is drained in the repetitious recital of mantras and hymns, and in performing innumerable meaningless rituals and ceremonies. They have been under the false belief that all these actions would directly deliver liberation. Shankara has unburdened us from this awful load we have been carrying and cautions us against wasting our hard-to-get human life on activities that are least helpful for our liberation. He freed us from superstitious concepts. He made it abundantly clear that neither any extraneous instrument nor any action will help in the realization of *brahman* and attainment of liberation.

This unequivocal enunciation of Shankara brings great relief to seekers. He simplified the path to Self-realization. Pilgrimages, rituals, mantra chanting, elaborate worships, and so on can be safely abandoned. There is no loss or danger in not performing any of them.

Knowledge is the Only Means

Shankara declares that Knowledge is the only means to attain the Self. Knowledge is the essential nature (*vastutantra*) of the Self, unlike rituals and worship (*puruShatantra*) that are dualistic in nature. Whether such actions (rituals/worship) are driven by our own intellect or by the scripture, they are motivated by intention or desire (*samkalpa*). Action, no action, or action of a specific nature are all motivated by intention.

As Shankara observes:

कर्तुमकर्तुमन्यथा वा कर्तुं शक्यं लौकिकं वैदिकं च कर्म; यथा
अश्वेन गच्छति, पद्भ्याम् , अन्यथा वा, न वा गच्छतीति।

Shankara in his commentary on
Brahma Sutras, I-i-2

If we have a desire to travel, we may decide to walk, ride a horse, or take a vehicle. We have such choices not only in our day-to-day activities but also in the activities prescribed by the scriptures. For example, although the scripture suggests using a particular type of vessel that has sixteen rims to perform a specific ritual called *ati rAtri*, it gives the ritualist the flexibility to choose another type of vessel, if necessary.

We have no such options on the Knowledge path. It is the intrinsic nature of Reality (Self) that determines everything, not the specific likes and dislikes of the seeker. Instead of expecting the Self to conform to the seeker's idea, the seeker must grasp the Self as it exists in its intrinsic nature. Reality does not change. Therefore, the Knowledge obtained from it also does not change.

viShayam or object is that which is perceived by us. It is also called "*pramEya.*" The means (*pramANa*) reveals the qualities (size, shape, etc.) of the object. When *pramEya* and *pramANa* are both available, the Knowledge of the substance is sure to take place.

For example, for us to become aware of a chair in the room, the chair must be present (*pramEya*), and our eyes (*pramANa*) must be able to perceive it. When the *pramEya* and *pramANa* are both present, it is impossible not to obtain the knowledge of the object. Even if the object has a certain orientation, our knowledge will conform to it and not differ from it. The knowledge of the object obtained from the eye proceeds to the retina and creates an impression (image) of the object in the mind. This modification in the mind is referred to by sages as *jnAna* (knowledge), *vRitti* (thought modification), *vRitti jnAna*, and so on.

"*brahman*" is a substance that is readily present. Like water, *brahman* too has specific features. The scripture describes the qualities of *brahman* in many ways:

नित्यशुद्धमुक्तस्वभावं ब्रह्मेति।
Shankara in his commentary on
Brahma Sutras, III-i-22.

"*brahman* is of eternal, pure, ever free nature."

यत्सर्वगतं सर्वान्तरं सर्वात्मकं च परं ब्रह्म
Shankara in his commentary on
Brahma Sutras, IV-iii-14.

"*brahman* is all-pervading, immanent, Supreme Self."

Like the eye that is the means to perceive objects, these descriptions of *brahman* are the means (*pramANa*) through which we can know the nature of *brahman*.

When our mind assumes the form of those attributes (eternal, pure, immanent, infinite, etc.) and a modification (*vRitti*) related to the *brahman* appears in our mind, it is called *brahmAkAra vRitti*.

Since Knowledge is intrinsic to the Self, it is *vastutantra*. Hence, it is not through logic and intellectual arguments, but only through the Knowledge of the Self that one can realize the Self.

There is another reason to consider Knowledge as the only means for attaining *brahman*. Most of the time, the means is driven by the goal to be achieved. The goal and the means must be of the same nature. A thorn can be removed with the help of another thorn. Only a diamond can cut another diamond. Hence, Knowledge is the only means to realize the Self whose nature is Pure Consciousness. *brahman* is non-different from Knowledge or Consciousness. The Upanishad holds,

प्रज्ञानं ब्रहम॥

Aitareya Upanishad, III-v-3.

"The Infinite Knowledge is *brahman*."

The above conclusion is reached from the viewpoint of *brahman*. It is also possible to reach the same conclusion from the viewpoint of the individual (*jIva*). The notion of a separate individual arises because of the beginning-less nescience. The individual forgets that his true nature is Consciousness and perceives himself as a finite being and the world as a separate entity. When ignorance is removed, the individual returns to his natural or original Self as *brahman*.

Knowledge (*jnAna*) is the antidote for removing ignorance (*ajnAna*). Ignorance is able to rule the roost because of the absence of Knowledge. Like the dawn that dispels darkness, Knowledge dispels ignorance. When ignorance is removed and Knowledge rises, the Self is automatically liberated.

Therefore, even from the perspective of the individual (*jIva*), the route to liberation is only through Self-Knowledge.

Negation of Objections

A few objections may be raised here. If Knowledge is the means to liberation and Knowledge implies "Knowing," isn't "Knowing" an action, a mental activity? Since we ruled out mental activity as a means to realize *brahman* earlier, how can we accept it now?

Secondly, what needs to be known is the nature of *brahman*. By "knowing" *brahman*, aren't we making *brahman* an "object" to our knowing? We have previously established that *brahman* is forever the subject. But it appears as though *brahman* has become an object in the process of our knowing It. This is contradictory to the nature of *brahman*, which is Pure Knowledge/Consciousness.

Shankara provides ingenious answers to these questions as well. He says, no means – karma, *upAsana,* or even *jnAna* – can help in attaining *brahman* because *brahman* is already present and is not something that must be acquired anew. The notion of attaining *brahman* (Self-Knowledge) is, therefore, a self-contradiction.

How can we then accept *jnAna* as a means to liberation? Shankara's answer is that the goal is not to "attain" Knowledge (Self), rather to use the Knowledge of the Self to negate and nullify the appearance of the not-Self (empirical world). Like darkness, the phenomenal world hides *brahman* from our sight. All that we need to do is to remove the veil (appearance of a world) of ignorance that hides *brahman*. Just as objects become visible when a torchlight is flashed into a dark room, Reality automatically reveals Itself the moment the veil of ignorance lifts.

Gist of the Scripture

We may wonder at this stage why the scripture discussed performing virtuous actions and worship when they are clearly not a valid means for realizing *brahman*. After all, it is the scripture itself that says Knowledge is the only means to attain liberation. Since the scripture teaches both *jnAna* and karma/*upAsana*, maybe the two paths are equally valid? How can one be right, while the other is wrong? Anticipating such an objection, Shankara gives an excellent response.

He says it is true that the scripture describes both *jnAna* and karma/*upAsana*, but it does so not because they both lead to liberation. It is only *jnAna* that leads to liberation. That is why Upanishads focus particularly on the Knowledge of the Self. The sections of the Vedas dealing with virtuous actions and worship are meant for the pursuit of *dharma* (righteousness). *dharma* is one of the four pursuits of human life prescribed by the scriptures. *dharma* refers to performing karma (actions) that is approved by the scripture. The result of such actions is the attainment of a heavenly abode after death.

People worship for many reasons. They pray to god for help in overcoming difficulties (*karmangopAsana*). They worship a favorite deity to attain wealth (*devatopAsana*) or worship *brahman* (*saguNa brahmOpAsana*) to achieve progressive or gradational liberation. Hence, all types of scripture-mandated actions or worship are in pursuit of *dharma* only, and not liberation. The results of such actions, at the most, may help the seeker attain heavenly abodes such as Satyaloka after death or secure for them a more comfortable rebirth on earth.

If we assess the fruits of such worship and actions properly, we realize that they only bind us and subject us to an endless cycle of birth and death, whether in this world or in another. They do not lead us to liberation.

A corollary question, in this context, could arise. The purpose of the scripture is to teach what is best for us. If it does not teach what is in our best interest, of what value is it? Of what use is *dharma* if it is incapable of liberating us? In fact, *dharma* seems to push us deeper into the mire of worldly life! Why did the scripture instruct on *dharma* in such detail, when *dharma* continues to keep us in bondage? It should have just taught us how to attain *mukti* (liberation), instead of teaching something contrary to *mukti*. How can we trust a text that contradicts itself?

Convergence

Shankara synthesizes all the contradictory statements in the scripture and provides the following profound answer. From a superficial viewpoint, it may appear as though the first part of the scripture (*karma kANda*) and the later part (*jnAna kANda*) contradict each other. The former seems to push us into duality and perpetuate *samsAra*, while the latter seems to lead us to the non-dual Supreme Bliss. Both seem to be separated by a big hiatus. If we, however, explore in-depth, we will find a great convergence between the two. Shankara says, karma and *upAsana* are not only useful for obtaining the limited results as stated earlier but can also be directed toward achieving liberation. To prevent a mighty river from wasting its waters by flowing into the ocean, we build dams and reservoirs to divert the water for irrigation and other developmental purposes. Similarly, we can direct the effect of karma and worship toward liberation, instead of *dharma*.

There are four types of karma or actions:

1. *nitya* or the prescribed holy actions of daily routine.

2. *naimittika* or actions performed on special occasions like eclipses, etc.

3. *kAmya* or actions performed with the desire for specific results.

4. *niShiddha* or prohibited actions.

Seekers of Self-Knowledge must refrain from performing the last two types of actions (*kAmya* and *niShiddha*). This will free them from the anxiety of attaining either heaven or hell after death. They can perform *nitya* and *naimittika* karma but must do so with a difference in attitude. They must perform these karmas as an offering to the Supreme Self without any sense of doer-ship or desire for particular results. Such an attitude will purify their mind and prevent them from accruing any negative results (demerits) from the karmas they perform. A purified mind is a mature field that is capable of receiving the Supreme Knowledge.

upAsana-s also, like karma, must be performed without any desire for specific results. Gods and goddesses must be worshiped as a manifestation of the Supreme Self. Such an attitude purifies the mind and improves its ability to concentrate on the Self.

Purification of the mind removes the veiling power (*tamas*) of nescience, while a concentrated mind obliterates the projection power (*rajas*) of nescience. With *rajas* and *tamas* removed, the *sattva* (pure) quality of the mind will shine forth brightly. This enables the seeds of Self-Knowledge to germinate in the mind of the seeker. The seeker will be able to directly experience the Knowledge of the Self.

In this manner, the *karma kANda* section of the Vedas also contributes to the liberation of the individual by helping the individual cultivate a pure mind that is capable of grasping the Self as it is. Hence, liberation is the ultimate goal of the karma and *jnAna* sections of the scripture. Shankara says:

एवं काम्यवर्जितं नित्यं कर्मजातं सर्वम्
आत्मज्ञानोत्पत्तिद्वारेण मोक्षसाधनत्वं प्रतिपद्यते; एवं
कर्मकाण्डेन अस्य एकवाक्यतावगतिः।

Shankara in his commentary on Brihadaranyaka
Upanishad, IV-iv-22.

116

Therefore, the purpose of the Vedas is to instruct on liberation. And the means for liberation is Knowledge only. This is the message that is conveyed in one way or the other by the scripture.

It is just incidental that the Vedas teach about karma first and later about Self-Knowledge. However, there should be no confusion, according to Shankara. The first part is only a pointer to the second part. Karma and *upAsana* are not an end in themselves. They prepare us for the second part, which focuses on Self-Knowledge. After performing karma and experiencing the results repeatedly, one develops detachment and dispassion for the material world and turns naturally toward Self-Knowledge.

One could argue that the scripture should have imparted the ultimate Knowledge in a straightforward manner rather than in an indirect way. The fault is not in the scripture but in the attitude of individuals. Some are extremely action-oriented. They think they have to "do" something to attain liberation. They are not drawn to the path of Knowledge, since it does not require any action.

There are others who worship *brahman* in one form or the other with a desire for a better life in this world or another. They hope to eventually attain liberation, which they think is superior to all kinds of happiness they have enjoyed so far. Such hopes and beliefs are strongly engraved in their minds, in spite of exhortations to the opposite by the scripture. Since the intention of the scripture is to benefit everyone without exception, it provisionally instructs such people to take up action (karma) and worship (*upAsana*) to satisfy their desires, although such actions are untrue and provide only transient happiness. After performing such actions and experiencing good and bad results for a while, individuals start introspecting and looking for ways to achieve lasting happiness. When they reach that point, the scripture presents them with the wisdom of the Upanishads.

Therefore, the scripture is not at fault. As Shankara says, the scripture is like a lamp. The lamp illuminates everything. Anything can happen in its light – good or bad actions or no actions. The lamp simply stands as a witness, untouched by action or inaction.

Another point to note is that people have different spiritual aspirations and capacities. The scripture caters to all of them in accord with their preferences. Even though it appears that the scripture is teaching something that is not perfect, its ultimate goal is to direct anyone who has developed dispassion toward liberation and impart the final Knowledge of the Self at the appropriate time.

Since Self-Knowledge is absolute, it stands as an uncontradictable doctrine. The entire discussion on karma must be considered an explication of an opposing theory. Self-Knowledge alone is established as the acceptable doctrine. Since the Upanishads form the quintessence of the Vedas, they are also known as Vedanta. Shankara declares with aplomb that Self-Knowledge is the ultimate teaching of the scriptures.

Scripture is the Only Means

There is yet another question that needs to be examined. Knowledge is said to be *vastutantra*. We refer to a thing as *vastutantra* if it depends on its own intrinsic qualities for its existence. We can clearly define and perceive any object that is external to us. As soon as we perceive it, a thought modification or an image of the object appears in our mind. We call that "knowledge" of the object. *brahman* is also a clearly defined substance. But It does not have a form, nor is It limited in time and space like worldly objects. It is universal, eternal, and immanent in all things. We are endowed with an intellect that can grasp It at all times. Thus, both the object (*pramEya*) and the means to know it (*pramANa*) are readily available to us. When both are available, there is nothing to prevent the Knowledge of the Self from arising in us spontaneously.

If the Knowledge of the Self can arise automatically, what is the necessity for the scripture? How can an inanimate thing like the scripture grasp and communicate Knowledge about the formless, changeless, indivisible *brahman*?

We can gain knowledge (*prama*) about a substance in two ways: through direct perception with the help of our sensory organs or through inference with the help of our mind. Knowledge about *brahman* is not something that we have to newly acquire. It is already available with us, although It is not "perceivable" like the worldly objects which we perceive with our mind and sense organs.

We can perceive anything as long as it is external to us, such as objects of sound, touch, shape, taste, and smell. Sometimes our perception may not be complete. We may see and perceive only a part of an object, and not all of it. Based on the parts we clearly perceive, our mind deduces that which is hidden from our direct perception. Deducing and knowing the remaining part with the mind is called inference. The entire finite world is known to us only through these two means – direct perception and inference.

However, *brahman* is not like the finite objects we perceive around us. Since It is the Self Itself, It is immeasurable. Because It does not have any label or form, the Self cannot be known by direct perception with our sensory organs. Neither can It be known by inference with our mind. Logicians introduced the concept of "indicators" (*linga*-s) for things that can be known by inference. For example, smoke is an indicator of fire. However, there are no such indicators for *brahman*. Hence, direct perception and inference are of no use in knowing *brahman*.

brahman is all-pervading and ever-present, and we have an intellect that can grasp It. Yet, we are unable to grasp It. How can we know *brahman* if the only two means we have are of no help? Shankara advises us to use the scripture like a lamp. A lamp does not create anything new; it simply reveals what is hidden from our perception. The substance *brahman* is already existing but is covered by the darkness of ignorance (lack of Self-Knowledge). So, we are unable to perceive It. If we dispel the darkness of ignorance with the light of Knowledge provided by the scripture, *brahman* reveals Itself.

Yet another objection may be raised. If the living intellect cannot know *brahman*, how can a lifeless scripture know It? The scripture is not merely a paper and a collection of letters and words. It is the essence of the truth experienced by ancient seers in higher states of Consciousness. The scripture is a textual rendition of such experience. Since direct experience is at the source of the knowledge of the scripture; it is not a lifeless entity. Since the knowledge is based on insights sages received during deep states of Consciousness (*samAdhi*), it is *vastutantra* only, and not *puruShatantra*.

According to Shankara, the scripture does not operate in the same manner as direct perception and inference. It does not reveal anything directly in positive terms. Instead, it uses the technique of negation. It negates the names and forms of the apparent world to reveal the underlying reality that is *brahman*. It removes the veil of ignorance and automatically reveals the Self. Since the scripture does not come into direct contact with the *brahman*, it does not affect the immeasurability (infinity) of *brahman* in any way. Since the scripture reveals the Knowledge of *brahman*, in this context, it may be said that *brahman* is an "object" that is "known" through the scripture.

It is absurd to say that the Self cannot be known! Self is what we are. Yet, why is it that we are unable to see It directly? It is because the not-Self, the phenomenal world, blocks the Self from our direct perception and makes it appear as though the Self is shining somewhere else!

Scripture is just a sound vibration. When the sound is uttered, it enters our mind through our ears. The mind grasps the meaning of the sound. An image commensurate with those impressions appears to the mind. In this way, the sound gets converted to a meaningful inference and the inference into direct perception. Thus, sound works like direct perception. Hence, we need not conceive *brahman* as something far from us. Even if the Self appears to be far away, the scripture can bring the Self close to us and make the illusory world that we perceive through direct perception and inference fade into the background. Hence, scripture is alive and not dead matter!

In fact, it is our senses and mind that are lifeless. Because they are associated with the separate self (*jīva*), they provide knowledge that is dependent on the separate self. Such knowledge is always associated with illusory phenomena. It cannot be the Absolute Reality. To know Reality as It IS, we must depend on Reality Itself. True Knowledge can come from the Upanishads only.

Self-Knowledge is the Only Practice

There is one final objection that we now need to address. We established that we are already *brahman*. We have also established that Reality-based Knowledge (*vastutantra*), not karma, is the only means for attaining the Knowledge of *brahman*. However, it feels like what we obtained so far is only intellectual knowledge – an idea or concept of *brahman*. A concept cannot be the real thing. Intellectual knowledge is not the same as experiential knowledge. Knowing how to build a house is not the same as building it. Knowing a recipe by rote is not the same as preparing and savoring the dish. Likewise, Knowledge about the Self is not the same as the experiential realization of the Self. When we think of something, an image of that thing appears in our mind. We refer to that image as knowledge of that "thing." Using the mental image as a clue, we can locate the real thing. Similarly, when we hear and reflect on the qualities of *brahman*, the knowledge or feeling of *brahman* arises in our mind. We then have to search and find the substance to which this Knowledge pertains.

Searching and finding are actions. But we said earlier that *brahman* cannot be known through action. However, it now appears as though *puruShatantra* must accompany *vastutantra* in order for us to realize *brahman*!

The scripture provides instructions on performing a ritual called *JyotiShToma*, but the instructions themselves are not the ritual. All the necessary materials and people must be assembled before we can start performing the ritual. We need to draw a plan of action and address questions such as what, whom, how, and so on. Hence, preparatory actions are necessary, in addition to the knowledge of the ritual. Knowledge needs to be converted into action in order to experience it. That is why the empirical world is said to be doer-dependent. It functions according to the desires of the individual.

Shankara counters the above argument. He says, such an objection makes sense in duality, but not in non-duality. In the relative world, experience of the object is different from the knowledge of the object. Since objects exist external to us, we can have a tactile experience of the objects.

The *shruti* says:

सर्वं तत्प्रज्ञानेत्रं प्रज्ञाने प्रतिष्ठितं प्रज्ञानेत्रो लोकः
प्रज्ञा प्रतिष्ठा प्रज्ञानं ब्रह्म॥
Aitareya Upanishad, III-v-3.

"All this is moved by Consciousness. The world is moved by Consciousness. The support is Consciousness. *brahman* is Consciousness."

विज्ञानमानन्दं ब्रह्म ...।
Brihadaranyaka Upanishad, III-ix-7.

"Knowledge, Bliss, is *brahman* ..."

This indicates that *brahman* is Knowledge and cannot be "known" like an object. What is "known" is the world. But the world is not different from *brahman*. How can we then search for *brahman* in the world? There is no world outside of *brahman*. *brahman* is both the Knower as well as the known. Hence, *brahman* is Perfection Itself!

Hence, the only means to realize *brahman* is through Self-Knowledge and nothing else. Since It is a single, undifferentiated, immutable substance, there is no room for anything else to exist, either a process, an action, or a performer of the action. The triad does not exist in *brahman*.

If the world continues to manifest even after we obtain Self-Knowledge, it is only due to our past karma (*prArabdha*). The only effort we need to make is to recognize all manifestation as Consciousness Itself. The Upanishad says:

तमेव धीरो विज्ञाय प्रज्ञां कुर्वीत ब्राह्मणः।
Brihadaranyaka Upanishad, IV-iv-21.

"The intelligent aspirant after *brahman*, knowing about this alone, should attain intuitive knowledge."

If obtaining the treasure of Knowledge is Intelligence, continuous abidance as that Knowledge is Wisdom. Shankara refers to it as *jnAna santAna karaNa,* which means the extension of Knowledge. We must live a life of single-minded focus on *brahman.* We cannot make it a karma (routine practice). It is not something that we have to search and find somewhere. Because Knowledge and the object of the Knowledge are one and the same, the Knowledge of *brahman* is not different from *brahman* or the experience of *brahman.* Hence, there is no special effort necessary to attain an immediated experience of *brahman.*

Knowledge Dispels Ignorance

The Upanishads only describe the nature of *brahman,* but not the path or means to attain It. Because of that, many naïve seekers imagine that there is a hidden path or means somewhere that they need to discover and practice in order to attain *brahman.* Carried away by such misconceptions, several unnecessary methods like mantra, *tantra,* yoga, *upAsana,* and so on have been developed. This is sheer indiscretion or imprudence. The scripture describes *brahman* from multiple angles directly and indirectly in the following manner:

सत्यं ज्ञानमनन्तं ब्रह्म।

Taittiriya Upanishad, II-i-1.

"Truth, Knowledge, and Infinity is brahman."

शुद्धं बुद्धं ..."Pure Awareness"

निष्कलं निष्क्रियं शान्तं निरवद्यं निरञ्जनम्।

Shvetashvatara Upanishad, VI - 19.

"Without parts, without activity, peaceful, without sound, without impurities, the supreme bridge to immortality, like a fire that burns without fuel, is He."

That is all the scripture does – describe the nature of *brahman*. When we hear the qualities of *brahman* described in such a manner, Knowledge of *brahman* rises in our mind. This Infinite Knowledge Itself is the intuitive experiential understanding of *brahman*.

To go to a particular village, a mere description of that village is not enough. We need directions to get to the village. The village is not the path. The village is the destination, and the directions are a means to get there. Hence, in addition to the description of the village, we also need instructions on how to reach it.

But Self-Knowledge is not like going to a village that is present in some distant location. *brahman* is everywhere. It is not different from us. Our essential nature (Self) cannot be objectified. We just need to understand the nature of our Self. The way to attain It is implied in It. There is no path outside anywhere (for you are already there). The means Itself is the end.

We travel in space to go from one place to the other. We travel in time from childhood to adolescence, from adolescence to adulthood, from adulthood to senility. Attainment of Self-Knowledge is not a similar movement in space or time. Shankara compares it to becoming healthy. Being healthy is our very nature. If we get ill, our health is temporarily masked. Administering medicine to get rid of the illness is all that we need to do. Once we get rid of the illness, we feel that we got our health back. Similarly, since our very nature is *brahman*, there is no question of acquiring It newly.

We are overtaken by a disease in the form of thoughts, such as "I am not That." As a result, our own natural state appears to be far from us. It is temporary amnesia. Like health hidden by an illness, our True nature is hidden by forgetfulness. All we need to do is to remove the layer of forgetfulness by means of the Knowledge provided by the scripture. By doing so, we will once again experience our natural intrinsic quality as *brahman*. Hence, attainment of Knowledge through the scripture is all that is required. That in Itself is an experiential understanding of the Self. We don't have to crave for some novel experience once we obtain the Knowledge of the Self.

No sooner do we light a lamp, darkness disappears and the existing objects become visible. Disappearance of darkness and appearance of objects happen simultaneously. There is no separate effort required to see the objects. In the same way, the moment the lamp called the scripture is lighted, the illumination called Self-Knowledge pervades and destroys the darkness of nescience, instantly giving us the experience of "I am *brahman*." According to Shankara, no other effort is necessary.

Conclusion

The essence of all the discussions above is that injunctions, actions, worships, eightfold yoga-s, *mantra*-s, *tantra*-s, and all other types of assorted knowledge are not an appropriate means to attain the Absolute Knowledge of *brahman*. That is because Absolute

Knowledge is an accomplished thing. The proper way to attain that Knowledge is to grasp it as it already is, and not depend on actions that are performed with a sense of doer-ship (*puruShatantra*). Self-Knowledge is reality-dependent (*vastutantra*), since Self is our essential nature; all other actions (karmas) are *puruShatantra* because they depend on human effort.

Knowledge of the Self does not arise just by itself. Valid sources of Knowledge are necessary. Direct perception and inference are the only two means that humans are equipped with. Both of these work well in the object-dependent illusory world but are of no use in obtaining the subjective Knowledge of the Self. Hence, scripture is the only valid means for attaining Self-Knowledge. The scripture provides that Knowledge through a process of negation rather than positive instruction. Therefore, *brahman* Knowledge is not an "object" for the scripture. It is enough to understand the nature of *brahman*. Then "What IS" will all be experienced as pervaded by *brahman*. There is no need to practice any routine (*sAdhana*), beyond attaining the Self-Knowledge provided by the scripture. Even if there is a need for some practice toward stabilization or abidance as *brahman*, it will only be a continuation of the *brahmAkAra vritti* (thought modifications in the form of *brahman*), and not karma or action.

Superimposition and Sublation

In the previous chapter, we stated that *vastutantra*, the knowledge based on the essential nature of the Self, is the only valid means of knowledge for realizing the Self. In this chapter, we will explore the various techniques the scripture uses to empower us with this knowledge.

Tat Twam Asi – You are That

The scripture declares the infinite nature of Consciousness in simple but profound statements. These declarations of the scripture are called *mahAvAkya-s*. There are four such declarations from the Upanishads, one from each of the four Vedas. Of the four, *tat twam asi* (You are That) and *aham brahmAsmi* (I am Pure Consciousness) are considered to be the most important declarations. *tat twam asi* is an instructional statement, while *aham brahmAsmi* is an experiential statement. What can be more profound than a teacher instructing a student on the truth, and the student experiencing the truth? Once the student experiences the truth, the teaching and the seeking come to an end. Therefore, it is said that these two great statements capture the essence of the entire scripture.

The result of deep contemplation on the *mahAvAkya*-s is the experience of the Self. Hence, according to Shankara, the statement *tat twam asi* is the foremost amongst the great sayings because it initiates the student into an investigation of the Self.

The statement *tat twam asi* translates into You are That, where *tat* means "That," *twam* means "You," and *asi* means "are." It declares that the individual is not different from Consciousness. Individuals (*jIvA-s*) labor under the misapprehension that they are separate from Consciousness. The scripture refutes such a notion and firmly asserts the truth that the individual is no different from Consciousness.

Sublation

The reasoning or logic the scripture uses to remove the misapprehension that the individual and Consciousness are separate is called *apavAda* (sublation or refutation). The scripture sublates the notion of a separate self and establishes the individual as non-different from Consciousness. As discussed in the previous chapters, the Indivisible Consciousness manifests in the human body without undergoing any change. Due to misidentification with the *upAdhi*-s, the mind-body adjuncts and the phenomenal world, It assumes the form of a finite individual even though It is Pure Infinite Consciousness. Once the adjuncts are transcended, the individual drops the notion of a separate self and once again experiences Self as Infinite Consciousness. Since the phenomenal world propagates the notion of a separate self, relentless practice of *apavAda* (sublation) is necessary to refute the phenomenal world. This is the essence of the great teaching – *tat twam asi*.

Several objections may be raised here. How can this vast micro and macro-cosmic world be sublated? Even if the scripture negates it, won't it continue to appear to us? Even if we negate it, how can it disappear? Even though it may not appear to us, it might appear somewhere else. If it appears in one place and not in another, then it must be fragmented. If it is fragmented, how can we experience It as the Undivided, Absolute Reality?

As discussed previously, it is due to the ignorance of our true nature that we imagine the phenomenal world to be real. Just like the water we perceive in a mirage, we perceive objects that do not really exist. Even after we know that the world is only notional, we continue to experience it. This is the nature of all appearances in the phenomenal world.

We cannot negate things that are inherently real, such as the blackness in an eyeliner. But we can negate things that appear as though they are real but are inherently unreal, such as the blackness in the night sky. The night sky appears black only due to misapprehension and not because the sky is inherently black. Hence, unreal appearances can be refuted. For instance, we will be scared if we see a snake in the dark. But the moment we look closely and recognize that it is a rope, we immediately drop the notion of a snake and see only a rope, and we are no longer afraid.

Similarly, this universe that we perceive as real does not have an existence of its own. However, due to primordial ignorance (lack of Self-Knowledge), we perceive a separate world out "there" and ourselves as finite individuals "in here." The moment the knowledge of the Self arises, ignorance disappears. When ignorance disappears, all appearances (world and individual) will dissolve, without a trace, into Consciousness because they were only imagined, to begin with! Absolute Consciousness alone IS. Hence, it is certainly possible to negate the universe, since its appearance is only imagined and not real.

Superimposition

The scripture suggests a two-step process to negate and dissolve the phenomenal world: 1) Superimposition (*adhyAropa*) 2) Sublation (*apavAda*). Superimposition is the process of imposing one thing on top of another. In the first step, the scripture superimposes a phenomenal world onto the substratum, which is Pure Consciousness. The superimposition, in this case, is only notional, since the thing that is superimposed is only imagined and does not actually exist. Shankara refers to such imagined superimposition as *adhyAropa*.

One may wonder why the scripture superimposes a world that does not exist on Consciousness. It is a natural tendency of the individual to perceive objects and not the substratum on which they appear. In accordance with this common experience, the scripture superimposes the phenomenal world on Consciousness.

Superimposition occurs in two ways. In the first instance, a sentient entity is superimposed on an insentient entity. The vital force (*prANa*) and the sense organs are insentient, but they appear to be sentient because they are permeated by Consciousness. This gives rise to body identification and the feeling "I am the body" (*dehAtmabhAva*). This is ego. Ego gives rise to the notion of "me," a separate self that perceives the world and transacts with it as "mine." This is the second instance of superimposition, where the insentient world (mine) is superimposed on a sentient individual (me), who perceives multiplicity (instead of non-duality) and suffers the consequences.

We may find it strange that the scripture superimposes an illusory world on Consciousness, instead of refuting it. If the scripture itself does so, why should the individual be blamed for superimposing the unreal on the real?

The scripture always tries to concur with common experience. The quintessence of its teaching is non-dual. It teaches that the world and the individual are unreal, and Consciousness alone is real. For this teaching to yield the expected results, we must grasp it "as is." But we fail to grasp it "as is" because our minds and tendencies are heavily conditioned by names and forms. For a mind that is conditioned to only perceive duality, the non-dual teaching is like a mirror in front of a blind person. It is of no use. Instead of trying to understand this truth, dualists argue that the non-dual teaching itself is wrong because it is contrary to their experience.

Therefore, although the essential teaching of the scripture is non-dual, to honor our common experience of the relative world, the scripture first describes the world as a superimposition on Consciousness, but later negates the superimposition and establishes Consciousness alone as the Absolute Reality. This is the strategy followed by the scripture.

Spontaneous Superimposition by the Individual

If it is the goal of the scripture to sublate the superimposed world, why doesn't it do so from the very beginning, instead of describing the superimposition and then explaining how to refute it? Shankara says there is a difference in the superimpositions made by the individual versus the one made by the scripture. Individuals spontaneously superimpose names and forms on Consciousness due to ignorance. They are not aware of the superimposition, nor of the process of removing it. So, they continue to engage with the world and succumb to the cycle of birth and death. They cannot get rid of the superimposition without the knowledge of the underlying reality, that is the Absolute Consciousness. Like the rope on which a snake is superimposed, Consciousness is the substratum on which the world is superimposed.

However, even though it is the substratum of everything, we do not perceive Consciousness because we are conditioned to only see multiplicity and not universality. Unless we are convinced beyond all doubt that the substratum of everything is Consciousness alone, we will continue to see duality. Only when we recognize the rope, the illusion of the snake will disappear. Once the knowledge of Consciousness as the Self arises, ignorance will disappear, and everything will appear as Consciousness alone. The scripture explains this truth using good reasoning and metaphors. Once we understand the truth, we will be able to grasp the underlying reality of all appearances "as is" and refute the superimposed world as an illusion.

Deliberate Superimposition by the Scripture

To establish that Consciousness is the substratum of everything that is perceived, the scripture first describes the world as a superimposition. The world appears like a ready-made product (effect). A product must have a producer (cause). It cannot manifest on its own. Every effect must have a cause. The scripture asserts that the Infinite Consciousness is the cause of the apparent world. The universe arises in, is sustained by, and merges back into Consciousness. The scripture describes Consciousness in vivid detail and contrasts it with the attributes of the world in an attempt to force our attention to go beyond names and forms to grasp the underlying reality that is Pure Consciousness. Instead of the not-Self (names and forms), our attention will then be drawn to the Self, which is Pure Consciousness. Therefore, although the phenomenal world in reality neither originates nor dissolves, the scripture first describes the world as being superimposed on Consciousness, so that it can later separate the world (effect) from the Consciousness (cause) in which it appears. If it does not describe the superimposition, our attention will be confined to the world and overlook the substratum on which it appears. Once we understand the nature of the superimposition, we will be able to refute the entire universe as unreal.

In this manner, the scripture first superimposes the world on Consciousness, separates it from Consciousness, reveals the underlying reality as Consciousness, and finally merges the world back into Consciousness. Consciousness is, therefore, both the instrumental and material cause of the world. When this understanding develops into a strong conviction, the world with its sentient and insentient objects disappears without a trace. We will be left with the feeling of Pure Non-Dual Consciousness.

The clay-pot metaphor clearly illustrates this concept. If we look casually at a pot, we will only notice its shape and not the substance it is made of. Although the substance (clay) is right in front of us in the shape of the pot, we will not notice it. In order to grasp the substance, we must separate the clay from the pot. We have to forget the roundness of the pot and focus instead on the common attributes of the clay, such as its blackness and hardness. Once we understand the characteristics of the substance, the form (pot) disappears and only the substance (clay) remains. We then realize that the pot is not different from the clay. Every bit of the pot is permeated with clay. If the pot breaks, the clay appears in a different form. In whatever form the clay appears, clay remains clay. Forms are unreal and only the substance that they are made up of is real. Once we understand that the world arises from and merges back into Consciousness, we realize that the effect is not different from the cause. The world is non-different from Consciousness.

Understanding the Differences

The scripture thus appropriately begins the teaching in duality and concludes in non-duality. The natural tendency of the individual to superimpose the world on Consciousness leads to bondage and the vicious cycle of birth and death. Just as a thorn is used to remove another thorn stuck in one's foot, the scripture uses the notion of superimposition to remove the superimposition made by the individual. It is only through this technique of superimposition and dissolution that we can directly experience Self as non-dual Consciousness. The great declaration *tat twam asi* (You are That), therefore, leads to the profound realization *aham brahmAsmi* – the experience of Self as Pure Consciousness.

The Experience of Consciousness

One may doubt whether it is possible to experience Pure Consciousness just by knowing a technique. Shankara assures us that it is quite possible. By contemplating deeply on the great declarations of the scripture, we obtain deep insights into our true nature. Shankara refers to these insights as the experience of the Self as Pure Consciousness. The statement *tat twam asi* states that the individual and Consciousness are non-different. When we hear such statements, we experience a feeling of expansiveness. That feeling itself is the experience of Consciousness.

Even after having such experiences of non-dual Consciousness, we doubt whether our experience is real. We find it hard to believe that our true nature is Consciousness and not a mind-body organism. As long as we only perceive names and forms, we will continue to experience ourselves as separate individuals and the world as a separate entity. Doubts about our Self as Pure Consciousness will continue to plague us. Relentless contemplation on the non-dual declarations of the scripture will help us develop a firm conviction that we are not the separate self that we perceive ourselves to be and that our true nature is Pure Consciousness.

It might be easier to believe that our essential nature is Consciousness, but harder to believe that the object world is unreal. Although we try to cultivate a non-dual outlook, the object world continues to persist and obstruct our progress. How can we then develop a firm conviction? We can develop such a conviction only if we contemplate on the *mahAvAkya*-s that declare that the individual and the world are not different from Consciousness. Although the individual's essential nature is also Consciousness, it is not absolute because the individual perceives himself or herself as a limited self and the world as a separate entity. By meditating on the great sayings, our consciousness will gradually expand into non-dual Consciousness. We will stop seeing names and forms, develop conviction that the world is an illusion, and start seeing Consciousness as Beingness (*sat*) and Knowingness (*cit*). As we mature in our practice, we will develop a strong conviction that Consciousness alone is real. We will stop seeing the world and ourselves as separate entities.

The phenomenal world is the *upAdhi* (adjunct) through which Consciousness manifests Itself. The individual feels separate from Consciousness because of the appearance of the world. The pot-space appears to be separate from the all-pervading space because of the appearance of the pot. If the adjunct (pot) is removed, the substance (space) alone remains. If the phenomenal world is removed, there is nothing anymore that separates the individual from Consciousness.

The individual will experience Self as Consciousness. There will no longer be any difference between the individual consciousness and the Absolute Consciousness.

Thought Modification in the Form of Consciousness

Different terms are used in Advaita to refer to the experience of the Self, such as *jnAnam and vidyA*. When we hear and understand the meaning of a word or sentence, a corresponding image arises in our mind. That image in the mind is called a *vRitti* or a thought modification. Any sentence could generate such an image. For instance, if someone describes a huge mountain, our mind assumes the form of the mountain, and the image of the mountain immediately appears in our mind. This is a natural tendency of the human mind. Therefore, when we reflect on the great sayings of the scripture that describe the Self as Pure Consciousness, our minds assume the form of that (Consciousness) which is being described, and we experience Self as the Infinite Consciousness (*akhandAkAra vRitti*).

It might be easy to conjure the images of the world, such as mountains and cities, because they have specific forms. But how can our minds conjure the image of something that is pure and formless, such as Consciousness?

Since Consciousness is the very nature of the Self, it is certainly possible to experience It even though It is formless, Shankara assures us. Consciousness is Knowingness. As individuals, we are self-aware, but our awareness is merged with names and forms, so it cannot be perceived distinctly. If the names and forms that veil the Self are removed, the Self will shine forth in all its splendor even though It is formless.

When names and forms, time and space are refuted, what remains is the Self as Pure Consciousness. Once we understand the truth, we need to hold on to it firmly and constantly remind ourselves of the truth. We simply know that we are tall or short, heavy or light without measuring ourselves constantly. Similarly, we must simply know that our true nature is Consciousness. Like the formless air and space that we cognize and the formless emotions that we experience, we can also experience Consciousness even though It is formless.

The Extraordinary Powers of the Mind

The human mind has extraordinary powers. It is like a two-edged sword. It has the capacity to analyze things as well as synthesize them. As an analytical mind, it is only capable of seeing many. As a synthesizing mind, with practice, over time, it can become subtle and capable of perceiving the underlying commonality that exists in all forms. For instance, an analytical mind will notice the flowers, fruits, leaves, and other parts of the tree, but not the tree as a whole. A synthesizing mind, on the other hand, will notice the tree as a whole and not its parts. It will notice the forest and not the tree. If we stretch this principle further, we find that even the forest loses its separate existence in the universality of the earth that contains mountains, rivers, and other objects. A synthesizing vision is a unifying vision. When we cultivate such a unifying vision, particulars dissolve and we perceive the underlying Universal Reality.

Earth and all its sentient and insentient entities are made up of the five elements — earth, water, air, fire, and ether. While the five elements are its particulars, touch, taste, sound, sight, and smell are its common attributes. Since earth contains all five of these attributes, it appears as a solid object. Since water loses smell and has only four attributes left, it is subtler than earth. Since fire loses both smell and taste and is left with only three attributes, it is subtler than water. In this manner, as we traverse from earth to ether, we find that each element progressively loses its attributes until, eventually, what remains is only sound (space). As a substance progressively gets attribute-less and subtler, it loses its form. When it loses its form, it becomes expansive. When it becomes expansive, it is all-pervasive.

The Self is infinitely larger than space. It does not have even sound for an attribute. It is devoid of all attributes; hence, It is the subtlest of all. Since It is extremely subtle, It is pure and all-pervasive. Self is the ultimate Universality within which all particulars, including the expansive space, dissolve without a trace. No object can exist separate from the Self, which is Pure Consciousness. In fact, it is Consciousness Itself that manifests as the object world, the not-Self. We perceive the not-Self as a separate entity because we lack the knowledge of the Self. The moment we refute the separate existence of the object world and recognize it as non-different from Consciousness, the object world will appear only as the Self. We will then experience the Self as Immediate and Infinite Consciousness. The five elements are the lowest level of particulars, while Consciousness is the highest level of commonality in this universe. The human mind is capable of grasping both these extremes, the lowest and the highest. For the mind to grasp an object, the object must have some attributes. Even though Consciousness does not have any attributes, when we hear the scripture describe It as Absolute, Infinite, and Pure, our minds attribute such qualities to Consciousness. Since all the qualities attributed to Consciousness are formless, with no boundaries, Consciousness can be summarized as Existence (*sat*). Existence or Beingness is a quality that pervades every object. When we hear these qualities described, our mind conjures up the vision of a formless, space-like, all-pervading Consciousness. This vision is the result of the individual's Consciousness in the form of the mind (Knowingness) merging with Existence (Beingness) in the form of space! Knowingness (*cit*) and Beingness (*sat*) are the essential nature of *brahman*, the Supreme Self.

It is the nature of the mind to assume the form of whatever object it reflects on. Just as the images of the mountains and rivers appear in our mind when we think of them, so also will the "image" of Consciousness with all its attributes appear in our mind. When the mind reflects on worldly objects, it develops an analytical outlook, so it only sees diversity. But when it reflects on the formless Consciousness, the mind synthesizes all forms and will only see the One underlying Reality.

स यो ह वै तत् परमं ब्रहम वेद ब्रह्मैव भवति

Mundaka Upanishad - 3.2.9

"He who knows that highest *brahman* becomes *brahman*."

The mind, therefore, has the capacity to assume either a fragmented or a unified outlook. It is not only capable of grasping names and forms, it can also grasp the Self as Knowingness and Beingness.

Because of its dualistic nature, the mind is often described as being both incapable and capable of realizing the Universal Self. The scripture describes both these aspects of the mind:

यन्मनसा न मनुते येनाहुर्मनो मतम्।
तदेव ब्रह्म त्वं विद्धि नेदं यदिदमुपासते॥

Kena Upanishad - 1.6.

"That which is not known by the mind but by which the mind is known, know That to be *brahman*."

मनसैवेदमाप्तव्यं ...।

Katha Upanishad - 2.4.11.

"By contemplation alone is the Self to be realized."

On the face of it, these statements might appear to be mutually contradictory. However, once we understand the nature of the mind, we realize that these are complementary, and not contradictory, statements. So long as the mind is object-oriented, it will see diversity and not commonality. It is in the context of such unrefined minds that the scripture says that the mind is not capable of realizing the Self. However, when the mind is sharpened by deep contemplation on the teachings of the scripture, it can transcend names and forms. Such a mind will be able to grasp the Self as Absolute Consciousness.

The scripture says that the refined mind is the only tool capable of helping us realize the Self.

A Caution about the Mind

Those with highly refined minds can grasp the Self "as is" by simply listening to the scripture. Unlike the not-Self objects of the world, Self has no attributes. Attributes such as existence/knowledge or space/mind are contrary to the essential nature of the Self, which is Pure Consciousness. Not everyone can grasp Consciousness directly just by hearing such descriptive terms. The descriptions might trigger a corresponding image in the mind. But the image would only be a fragmented view of the Absolute. When the scripture says that Consciousness is like space, it is only trying to give us a metaphor to help us imagine an aspect of Consciousness. It is not, however, trying to limit Consciousness to space! Instead of using these attributes as a means to reach the end, the ultimate experience of the Self, the mind gets attached to the attributes and starts treating them as the end! Instead of grasping Consciousness as formless, it ends up objectifying Consciousness. Hence, Shankara cautions seekers about using their mind to directly grasp Consciousness "as is," since the mind has a natural tendency to objectify things.

Shankara advises us instead to take an indirect approach – the process of negation. Negation is synonymous with dissolution. It is the process of eliminating one thing after the other till nothing but the truth remains. This is the *neti neti* (not this, not this) path advocated by the Upanishads. Shankara provides multiple reasons for why the scripture uses the word *neti* twice. The first utterance, he says, is to negate the manifested world made up of the five elements and the second is to negate the un-manifested world (dormant tendencies). He also says *neti* is used twice to reinforce the complete negation of everything that is perceived in this universe without exception. When everything that the mind perceives is discarded as unreal and there is nothing else left in the universe, what remains is Consciousness alone. Once the mind reaches the conclusion that the Self alone IS, it comes to a complete rest, with no more desire to seek. It experiences the Self as Pure Consciousness.

Names and forms (not-Self) prevent us from experiencing the Self. Once we refute their appearance as unreal, the underlying Consciousness will shine forth as the Self. Consciousness is not somewhere far from us. Like space, Consciousness permeates everything. It is both inside and outside us. It is our very nature, so we cannot get rid of it. It is also not something that we need to acquire or get closer to, since it is already present everywhere, including where we are right now! Therefore, there is no effort required to attain the Self since it is ever-present. The effort required is only to remove the not-Self that is falsely superimposed on the Self.

Dissolution (*pravilApana*)

The term *pravilApana* has a special meaning and significance in Advaita, which is different from its colloquial usage. In colloquial usage, *pravilApana* means "discarding." If something is discarded, it means it is not present here at the moment, but it might be present somewhere else. It does not disappear altogether. But the process of *pravilApana* in Advaita implies that when a thing is negated and discarded, it disappears altogether without a trace. It completely loses its separate existence. Shankara referred to this practice as total dissolution, the complete melting away of things. The Self is Pure Consciousness, but it appears solidified as the phenomenal world. The world is "melted away" completely through the practice of *pravilApana* in Advaita. As a result, the world loses its apparent solidity, and the Self alone remains.

This process of "melting away" is not like the melting of a solid substance into liquid or of butter into ghee. Although the world appears as a solid object, it cannot be melted away using any physical means. It can be done so only through Self-Knowledge. Since we lack the knowledge of the Self, we perceive names and forms instead of the Self, which is Pure Consciousness. This ignorance is beginning-less and has persisted over lifetimes. Since it is beginning-less, its roots are deep and get stronger with every birth and death cycle. Just like the disappearance of darkness when the sun rises, so also will ignorance disappear when Self-Knowledge arises.

Knowledge is a mental process, but the world is physical matter. One may wonder how knowledge can melt matter. We ask, how can the world disappear, just by us dismissing its existence mentally? Shankara tells us that it is possible to dissolve the world with Knowledge, since the world is just an illusion. He asks us to consider the experience of the dream world. Objects in the dream appear solid, and we experience them as real in the dream state. The moment we wake up from the dream, the dream objects that had appeared so real disappear without a trace. It is only due to ignorance that we imagined the dream objects to be real.

The world we perceive in the waking state is also a dream! None of the events, people, or situations we experienced a few years ago are present today. All we have are memories of the past. People and situations we experience today will fade away into memory in a few years. Life feels like a dream when we realize how forms and events dissolve effortlessly in time. That is why the Upanishads describe all three states – waking, dream, and deep sleep – as a dream!

The Necessity to Superimpose

Although events and people disappear in the course of time, the sentient and insentient world continues to appear to us in one form or the other. It will never completely disappear and leave a void behind. Even though familiar forms disappear over time, other objects, time, and space will continue to appear. When the three dimensions – objects, time, and space – continue to manifest in infinite ways, is it ever possible to dissolve them? non-dual aspirants are often plagued by such doubts.

Shankara says such doubts will continue to persist if we try to negate the superimposed world without grasping the substratum on which it appears. The snake will disappear only after the rope is perceived, and not by simply wishing the snake to go away. Shankara says:

दृष्टिं ज्ञानमयीं कृत्वा पश्येद्ब्रह्ममयं जगत्।

Aparokshanubhuti, 116

"If we perceive the world from the viewpoint of Consciousness, the world will appear as Consciousness."

Therefore, in order to get rid of the illusory appearance of the world, we must acquire the knowledge of the substratum on which it appears. The substratum can be recognized only by understanding the nature of the superimposition.

Like the gold that permeates the entire ornament, Consciousness permeates everything in the phenomenal world. It is so tightly integrated into everything that it is difficult to separate It from the world. Just like the forms of the ornaments appearing in the forefront and not of the gold that they are made up of, worldly objects appear in the forefront, not Consciousness. Consciousness not only recedes into the background, but It also appears as names and forms, making it difficult for us to grasp It. We can overcome this problem only by discerning Consciousness from the objects that are superimposed on It and recognizing Its essential nature. The scripture says that Consciousness is the cause of the apparent world, therefore Its characteristics are different from those of the creation. Creation is full of forms, but Consciousness is formless. Forms are limited, but Consciousness is Infinite. Hence, it is possible to differentiate Consciousness from the phenomenal world by recognizing Its characteristics, such as Formlessness, Unknowability, and Infiniteness.

As soon as we hear this description of Consciousness, we immediately experience a space-like, no-boundary expansiveness. The scripture refers to this experience as *brahmAkAra vRitti*, a thought modification in the form of Consciousness. This thought modification is the knowledge of Consciousness. Such knowledge is the result of the understanding that the phenomenal world is a superimposition on Consciousness. Once we have the knowledge of the substratum, we will no longer perceive the superimposed world as real. Objects will lose their separate existence, and the world will appear uniformly as Beingness (*sat*) and Knowingness (*cit*). All forms merge into Consciousness, and the Self alone remains.

Hence, although dissolution is the ultimate goal, superimposition is the first step. While superimposition reveals the substratum, dissolution dissolves the world into the substratum. A contention may be raised here. Can the Self be grasped by a mere thought modification, especially if the experience of the Self is fleeting? Shankara says, even though the feeling of *brahman* or the experience of Consciousness is fleeting, it is enough to initiate the process of dissolution. Like the thorn that is used to remove another thorn and is later discarded, the experience of *brahman* is used to trigger the process of dissolution. When names and forms dissolve into Consciousness, so will the feeling of *brahman*. Self alone remains.

The Superimposition and Dissolution Process

The superimposition and dissolution process is designed as a practice to facilitate the experience of the Self in the student.

This is an age-old practice that has been handed down from the teacher to the student. Shankara declared that this is the only method for teaching Vedanta.

Shankara's monumental works, the commentaries on the Upanishads, Brahma Sutras, and Bhagavad Gita, are based on this very principle. Advaitins consider dissolution (*apavAda*) as the primary instruction and superimposition (*adhyAropa*) as a secondary instruction. The *mahAvAkya*-s, like *tat twam asi*, destroy the illusory appearance of the world and bestow the experience of Consciousness. All other statements describing the phenomenal world are extraneous and secondary to the *mahAvAkya*-s.

The extraneous descriptions of the superimposed world provide object knowledge. Object knowledge is false, since it describes the non-dual Consciousness in dualistic terms. Through a process of analysis, we can separate names and forms from the Consciousness that permeates them. The primary goal of the scripture is to synthesize the differences and reveal the single underlying reality as Consciousness. It uses the object knowledge as a means toward that end.

Shankara illustrates this concept through the story of a young prince who lost his father in the war. To protect the prince from the enemies, the king's minister takes the prince to a tribal village and leaves him in the care of a village elder. The prince grew up as a tribal boy with no knowledge of his royal lineage. On his death bed, the village elder calls the boy to his bedside and tells him the truth about his royal birth. He tells the prince to fight his enemies and claim his kingdom back. As soon as he hears the truth about his birth, the boy drops all his attachment to the tribal village and develops an attachment to his kingdom.

The individual (*jīva*) is like the prince in the story. Due to the effects of past actions (karma), the individual takes birth, performs actions, and experiences the results of his actions. He goes through the vicious cycle of births and deaths until he meets a realized master who reveals to him the truth about the Self. The individual first realizes that Self is Pure Consciousness and later realizes that the phenomenal world is not different from the Self. The scripture describes the creation and dissolution of the world, the birth and death of the individual, and other such polarities only to point out their illusory nature and to promote a non-dual vision. Paper, ink, and pen are tools that help us write and understand the meanings of words and numbers. They are neither the words nor numbers themselves, but only the means by which words and numbers can be expressed and understood. Once their purpose is served, the tools can be discarded.

Similarly, the scripture provides descriptions of the creation and dissolution of the world only to help us understand the underlying non-dual reality, and not because creation and dissolution actually happened. Once we attain the Knowledge of the Self, these aids (object world) are no longer necessary. We cannot discard them like the pen and paper in the previous analogy, since they are not real. They simply dissolve into the Self when the Knowledge of the Self arises. We then experience our Self as Absolute Consciousness.

Therefore, even though the scripture describes the phenomenal world, such descriptions are false. They only point to the truth and are not the truth itself. In other words, superimposition is invoked only to culminate in the process of dissolution. Shankara constantly reminds us that this is the only method for experiencing the Self. The Upanishads use the same strategy. They first superimpose a phenomenal world on Consciousness and then sublate or negate it. Each Upanishad, however, reveals a different aspect of this process. Let us see how in the following section.

Strategy of the Scriptures

The Aitareya and Chandogya Upanishads first describe creation, then its dissolution, and eventually dismiss both as unreal. The Prasna Upanishad first describes how energy and matter originated and evolved into the phenomenal world, but eventually dissolves them both into the Self. The Taittiriya Upanishad first describes the evolution of Consciousness into the five sheaths (body, vital force, mind, intellect, and bliss), then explains how Consciousness transcends the five sheaths, and finally concludes that the five sheaths are non-different from Consciousness and therefore are non-existent. The Brihadaranyaka Upanishad first presents particulars about the phenomenal world in great detail, gradually negates each description, and finally reveals the common underlying reality, which is the substratum of the phenomenal world. The Katha Upanishad describes the body, mind, and other adjuncts in detail, systematically classifies them into gross and subtle matters, and gradually draws our attention to the most subtle substance of all, which is the Self. The Mandukya Upanishad first describes the three states of Consciousness (wakeful, dream, and deep sleep) and finally merges them into Consciousness (*turiya*), which is imminent in and transcends all states.

Every Upanishad first declares that there is only one reality, which is Absolute and Non-Dual. Later, anticipating questions from the students, it projects and superimposes a relative world on the Absolute Reality. Eventually, it refutes the superimposed world as not real, and once again concludes that there is only One Reality, which is Absolute and Non-Dual.

For instance, the Chandogya Upanishad, at the very beginning, declares the non-dual nature of Consciousness.

सदेव सोम्येदमग्र आसीदेकमेवाद्वितीयम्।
तद्धैक आहुरसदेवेदमग्र आसीदेकमेवाद्वितीयं
तस्मादसतः सज्जायत॥
Chandogya Upanishad - 6.2.1

"In the beginning, this universe was Being (*sat*) alone, one only without a second. Some say that in the beginning, this was non-being (*asat*) alone, one only without a second; and from that non-being, being was born."

Later, it describes the creation of the individual and the world in great detail. Eventually, to make sure we don't assume that the world and the individual are real, it once again declares that Consciousness alone is real, and the entire creation is false.

स य एषोऽणिमैतदात्म्यमिद सर्वं तत्सत्य स
आत्मा तत्त्वमसि॥

Chandogya Upanishad - 6.8.7

"That which is the subtlest of all is the Self of all this. It is the Truth. It is the Self. That thou art."

Even the Bhagavad Gita and the Brahma Sutras, which are an amplification of the Upanishads, follow the same pattern. The second sutra (aphorism) in the Brahma Sutras, for instance, superimposes the entire creation on Consciousness.

जन्माद्यस्य यतः ॐ॥

Brahma Sutras - 1.1.2

Later, in another sutra, it dismisses the creation as unreal and reveals Pure Consciousness alone as real.

तदनन्यत्वमारम्भणशब्दादिभ्यः॥

Brahma Sutras - 2.1.14

मया ततमिदं सर्वं जगदव्यक्तमूर्तिना।
मत्स्थानि सर्वभूतानि न चाहं तेष्ववस्थितः॥

Bhagavad Gita 9-4

"This entire world is pervaded by me, by my un-manifest form. All beings reside in me, but I am not bound in them."

न च मत्स्थानि भूतानि पश्य मे योगमैश्वरम्।
भूतभृन्न च भूतस्थो ममात्मा भूतभावनः॥

Bhagavad Gita 9-5

"Nor do all beings reside in me. Behold my majestic power. Sustaining beings without being bound to them is myself, giving existence."

Had the scripture described the non-dual reality only from the very beginning, we would not have grasped it because our minds are conditioned to only see the relative reality.

It is not enough to simply negate names and forms. The negation must be done based on the knowledge of the substratum. That is the reason why the scripture does not simply refute the existence of the object world but explains that its appearance is not real. This implies that the world appears only if Consciousness is present. If Consciousness is absent, the world will not appear because the world has no separate existence of its own.

Removal of Lingering Doubts

Based on previous discussions, it is evident that superimposition is a necessary process because it reveals the knowledge of the substratum. The knowledge of the substratum leads to the dissolution of the world. The great teaching *tat twam asi* leads to the realization and the experience of *aham brahmAsmi*. When the individual stops feeling "I am the body" and starts feeling "I am Consciousness," that is the experience of *aham brahmAsmi*. There is no doubt that such an experience of the Self is possible, says Shankara. Emotions, such as joys and sorrows, do not enter Pure Consciousness. If they enter, they become Consciousness Itself and not an object for Consciousness to experience. Shankara says that the feeling "I have no sorrow or happiness. I am Pure Consciousness" is the experience of the Self. When all emotions dissipate and Self alone remains, the object world disappears. With the disappearance of the object world, the notion of a separate self also disappears. When the world and the individual disappear, we experience our very nature (Self) as Pure Consciousness.

Doubts might still persist. This body-mind organism and the huge universe seem to conceal Consciousness. Isn't it just solipsism to think that the Self alone exists? Shankara says such questions are meaningless because the dissolution of the world is not a mere mental process. It is a process by which every object of knowledge is systematically eliminated (*neti neti*) until what remains is Pure Knowing or Consciousness alone. Hence, the experience of Consciousness is not an illusion created by the mind. It is the true knowledge of the Self.

"It might be true knowledge, but how does it benefit me?" we may wonder. "Why would the scripture discuss it if there was no benefit?" Shankara counters. The scripture would have been silent rather than waste our time if there was no benefit. Even a foolish person will not do anything without a specific purpose for doing it. The scripture, which is the source of the highest knowledge, has a very clear purpose. Its purpose is to liberate us from misery (ignorance) and establish us in bliss (Self). It assures us that such liberated beings exist even today. So, it is possible even for us to attain lasting bliss and peace.

Superimposition and dissolution are the only practice that can help us attain such lasting bliss and peace. By reading and reflecting on the teachings of the scripture, we acquire the knowledge of the Self, and this knowledge, in turn, facilitates the experience of the Self as Pure Consciousness. While the great saying *tat twam asi* provides the knowledge of the Self, the saying *aham brahmAsmi* provides the experience of the Self. These two *mahAvAkya*-s bestow the ultimate benefit on us and help us achieve the purpose of our human existence.

Conclusion

To realize the ultimate purpose of human existence, we must acquire the right knowledge. The great teachings of the scripture (*mahAvAkya*-s) offer such knowledge. By instructing us on the process of superimposition and dissolution, the scripture reveals to us the knowledge of the Self. Since we cannot grasp the non-dual nature of the Self directly, the scripture separates the phenomenal world from Consciousness and describes it as a superimposition on Consciousness. Later, using higher reasoning and analogies, it refutes the appearance of the phenomenal world and proves that the world is non-different from Consciousness. When we understand this truth, a thought modification (*vRitti*) in the form of expansive Consciousness is generated in our mind, which results in the experience of the Self as Pure Consciousness. The great instruction *tat twam asi* (You are That) culminates in *aham brahmAsmi,* the experience of the Self as Pure Consciousness. Joy and sorrow are completely annihilated. Not a trace of ignorance remains. The experience of the Self as Pure Consciousness is natural to us since it is our very nature. It is not an acquired state. The *mahAvAkya*-s remind us of this truth.

Action and Knowledge

In the last two chapters, we discussed the process (*sAdhana*) of self-inquiry. We concluded that knowledge is the only means for realizing the Self and discussed how such knowledge can liberate us from ignorance and bondage. We also concluded that in-depth knowledge of the Self is in itself the direct experience of the Self. In this chapter, we will discuss various *sAdhana*-s (practices) and how they help us in our efforts to attain Self-Knowledge.

If knowledge of the Self is indeed the direct experience of the Self, whoever hears the teaching should be able to attain the knowledge and experience of the Self. However, we don't see any evidence of that happening. We can't even be sure if even one among a thousand who hear the teaching will understand the nature of the Self, let alone experience it! Even people like us, who have been listening and reflecting on the teaching for years, don't seem to be making much progress. At the most, we might have attained some knowledge of the object world and some knowledge of the scripture, but not true Self-Knowledge. If we had really attained Self-Knowledge, we would not be caught up in this worldly existence or *samsAra*. From the very fact that we continue to be caught up in *samsAra*, it is evident that we are far from attaining Self-Knowledge. When the

Self, whose nature is Pure Consciousness, is all-pervading and freely available, when the scripture, the supreme source of knowledge, is readily available, and when we have an intellect that is capable of understanding the truth, why is it that we continue to fail to grasp the Self?

When all the necessary ingredients are available, it should be easy to cook a dish. But if we fail to do so, it must be either due to a flaw in the ingredients or some other obstruction. As discussed in the previous chapters, there can be no flaw in the ingredients for realizing the Self, which are Consciousness, scripture, and our intellect. According to Shankara, the only reason why we fail to grasp the Self even though all the necessary ingredients are present is due to *prArabdha* karma, the results of our past actions.

Karma

What is this karma, and how does it prevent us from attaining Self-Knowledge? Karma refers to the actions we perform. We are constantly engaged in one activity or the other with our body and mind. We cannot rest even for a minute without engaging in some task or the other. For instance, we inhale and exhale continuously. These actions arise and subside spontaneously on their own, so we do not have to pay much attention to them. However, instead of simply accepting these as spontaneous actions, we take ownership. We perform actions assuming we are the doers and enjoyers of the results. Every action has a reaction. These reactions leave deep impressions in our mind. These impressions or tendencies are called *vAsanA*-s or *samskAra*-s. It is these *vAsanA*-s that contribute to the inequality and diversity we perceive in the phenomenal world. They cannot be avoided or ignored. They are beginning-less and endless. They continue in the subtle form even after the gross body perishes. We cannot assume that they do not exist just because they are not visible to our naked eye. We do not see our life-force (*prANa*) or the mind (*manas*) either, but we know they exist in invisible form. In the same way, these beginning-less impressions continue to exist in a subtle form from one birth to another. Shankara says, like the smell of asafetida that persists in the cloth even after it is removed from the cloth, *vAsanA*-s persist in the subtle form even after the individual (*jIva*) discards the physical body.

Results of Past Actions (*prArabdha*)

Over lifetimes, tendencies transform into instincts. Since they are acquired over many lifetimes and are countless in number, they are called *sancita* or accrued karma. When some of the *sancita* karma comes to fruition and starts operating, it is called *prArabdha* karma, or karma that is in motion. It is due to *prArabdha* karma that we attained this birth. It is *prArabdha* karma that defines how long we live, what actions we perform in this life, what joys and sorrows we experience, what sort of thoughts and ideas we entertain, what words we utter, and so on. However, we don't simply experience the results of our past actions in our current life. We simultaneously also create new karma with our actions. This new karma that we generate in the current birth is called *AgAmi* karma. *AgAmi* karma gets added to the previously accrued *sancita* karma. Hence, *AgAmi* karma generates *sancita* karma, *sancita* karma generates *prArabdha* karma, and *prArabdha* karma generates *AgAmi*. As karma continues to accrue endlessly, the *jIva* continues to be burdened endlessly by the weight of accrued karma.

We have spent many births caught up in this vicious cycle of karma, but we are now determined to break ourselves free of this cycle and attain Self-Knowledge. *prArabdha* karma is operating everywhere. It has been present long before we began our efforts to attain Self-Knowledge. Since karma precedes all our efforts to attain Self-Knowledge, it is much stronger than our desire for Self-Knowledge. Therefore, karma overpowers and surpasses our efforts to attain knowledge and experience the Self. It is due to this overwhelming power of karma that we fail to attain Self-Knowledge even when all the necessary ingredients are available. As long as *prArabdha* karma is operating, our mind will flow only toward the external world and not inwards toward the Self. If the mind does not flow inwards, how can the Knowledge of the Self arise in us? Hence, according to Shankara, it is *prArabdha* karma only that prevents us from experiencing the Self.

Is there a solution to this problem? If everyone is subject to *prArabdha* karma and *prArabdha* karma is eternally present, is there any scope for anyone to attain Self-Knowledge? Shankara says that there certainly is a solution, and the scripture provides it. The scripture and the teaching would be a total waste if they do not benefit anyone.

Listen, Contemplate, and Meditate

The scripture offers the three-fold practice as the solution: *shravaNa* (listen), *manana* (contemplate), and *nididhyAsana* (meditate). In the Brihadaranyaka Upanishad, before walking away into the forest as a renunciate, Sage Yagnyavalkya tells his wife Maitreyi to live comfortably with the wealth he had given her. Maitreyi asks him if wealth will help her attain immortality. The sage laughs and tells her that it is only Self-Knowledge that can help her, and no amount of wealth can help her attain immortality. Upon hearing this, Maitreyi rejects the wealth and asks the sage to initiate her in a practice (*sAdhana*) that will help her attain Self-Knowledge. Sage Yagnyavalkya then tells her to perceive everything as Self alone and to constantly listen, contemplate, and meditate on the Self.

न वा अरे सर्वस्य कामाय सर्वं प्रियं भवत्यात्मनस्तु
कामाय सर्वं प्रियं भवत्यात्मा वा अरे द्रष्टव्यः
श्रोतव्यो मन्तव्यो निदिध्यासितव्यो। मैत्रेय्यात्मनो वा अरे
दर्शनेन श्रवणेन मत्या विज्ञानेनेद सर्वं विदितम्॥5॥ -
Brihadaranyaka Upanishad Ch 2

"O, Maitreyi, it is the Atman that is to be beheld; it is the Atman that is to be known; it is the Atman that is to be searched for; it is the Atman which is to be heard about; it is the Atman which is to be thought in the mind; it is the Atman which is to be meditated upon. There is nothing else worthwhile thinking, nothing else worthwhile possessing, because nothing worthwhile exists, other than This."

Immortality, liberation from the vicious cycle of birth and death, is only possible through Self-Knowledge. This is the ultimate goal of human life. Only by listening to the scripture describe the nature of the Self, contemplating on the Self continuously, and meditating on the Self with single-pointed concentration can one attain Self-Knowledge. This three-fold practice removes the effects of past karma and purifies the mind. When a purified mind hears the *mahAvAkya*-s (the great declarations of the scripture), such as *tat twam asi*, it immediately grasps the nature of the Self. Therefore, even when *prArabdha* karma is operating, relentless practice (*shravaNa, manana, nididhyAsana*) will remove the effect of the past karma and cultivate a pure mind that is capable of grasping the Self.

Let us now understand how practice removes *prArabdha* karma and culminates in Self-Knowledge. The first step in the practice is *shravaNa*, to listen and understand the meaning of the *mahAvAkya*-s, such as *tat twam asi* (You are That). These *mahAvAkya*-s describe the nature of the Self as Pure Infinite Undivided Consciousness. When we hear these declarations of the scripture, we become aware of an entity called Consciousness. We typically are only aware of the phenomenal world around us. Because we experience the world directly with our senses, we do not question or doubt its existence. We are not aware of Consciousness because we do not perceive it with our senses. It is only the *mahAvAkya*-s that reveal the existence of Consciousness.

The scripture describes Consciousness as Existence, Knowledge, and Infinity – *satyam-jnAnam-anantam brahma*. The term "Existence" suggests that Consciousness exists even though we do not perceive it directly. Consciousness is the basis of the entire world we perceive. If we think the world exists, we must also consider the substratum on which it exists. Without the substratum, the world will cease to exist. But we perceive the world and every object in it as existing, not as non-existing!

What is the nature of this substratum on which the phenomenal world appears? The Upanishad describes it as *jnAna* or Consciousness (Knowledge). Hence, Consciousness is the knower of all objects and not an object that can be known or perceived like the objects of the world.

What is the nature of this Consciousness? Upanishad uses a third attribute, *anantam* (Infinite), to describe it. The moment we perceive an object, our knowledge gets fragmented and limited to the object we perceive. A thing becomes limited when there is another thing that encroaches on it. If there is only one thing, it is infinite, with no limits. Consciousness is Infinite, one without a second, so It has no boundaries and no trace of duality in It.

When we hear the scripture describe the nature of the Self as Pure Consciousness, our mind assumes the form of Consciousness (*brahmAkAra vRitti*), and the corresponding knowledge of the Self arises in our mind. With the arising of Self-Knowledge, ignorance is dispelled, and the Self is experienced as Infinite Consciousness.

Even after ignorance is dispelled and Self-Knowledge arises, we continue to have doubts. It is easier for us to accept that Self is Consciousness, but harder to accept that It is undivided and non-dual. If it is non-dual and undivided, why do we see many and not the One? Why do we continue to see multiplicity and not commonality? How can we develop a strong conviction that the Self is Infinite Consciousness?

To remove such doubts, the scripture suggests the next step in the practice – *mananaM* or contemplation. Contemplation on the teaching must progress in the form of good reasoning, with the help of examples that clearly illustrate the point. Once we listen to the *mahAvAkya*-s describe the nature of the Self, with the help of sound reasoning and examples, we must dig deeper into their meaning. Without such in-depth analysis, we will continue to doubt the existence and infinite nature of Consciousness. We have to understand that the apparent world is only an illusion, a reflection of the real substance, which is Consciousness. Just like the rope that appears as a snake, Consciousness Itself appears as the object world. Once we understand and accept this as a fact, we will realize that the object is not different from the substance it is made of. The snake does not have a separate existence from the rope. Similarly, the phenomenal world does not exist separate from Consciousness. It arises from and merges into Consciousness; hence, it is not different from Consciousness. Inquiry into the nature of the Self must progress in this manner. Even though the object world appears as a separate entity, unless every object is illumined by our Consciousness, we do not become aware of it. Unless it is illumined by our Consciousness, an object has no existence. Once we realize that the object world has no separate existence from Consciousness, we find our Self as

Consciousness, expanding and permeating everything. Once we analyze and understand that Consciousness alone is, all doubts vanish.

Even after we are convinced that Consciousness alone is real and the object world is unreal, we might think it is just an intellectual understanding since we continue to perceive the world. How can we accept that Consciousness is undivided and infinite if we continue to see duality? If we continue to see duality even after acquiring the knowledge of the non-dual Self, Shankara says, it is only due to *viparyayam* or misapprehension. We may have an intellectual appreciation of the non-dual reality, but do not have the direct experience of the Self. The moment we loosen our grasp on the non-dual Self, we once again start perceiving the heterogeneous world as real. When such heterogeneous feelings arise, the homogenous feeling of non-duality ceases. Therefore, we must strive to develop an uninterrupted homogeneous vision that is not distracted by the multiplicity of the phenomenal world. When we develop such a homogenous vision, the Knowledge of the Self will no longer be mere intellectual knowledge. It will transform into a stable and abiding experience of the Self. This is called *nididhyAsana. nididhyAsana* removes *viparyayam (*misapprehension). We will no longer experience an inside and an outside world. We will continuously experience only the Self as Infinite Consciousness. In such a state of Consciousness, all objects and transactions with the world will also appear as arising and merging in Consciousness. Everything that we see, hear, and touch – everything that we grasp with our senses – will lose its separate existence and will appear only as Pure Consciousness. Our mind will become possessed by such non-dual feelings.

If we sincerely follow the three-fold practice (*shravaNa, manana, nididhyAsana*), the impact of *prArabdha* karma will eventually fade away, leaving our minds pure and tranquil. With a purified mind, we will be able to grasp the Self as It is, and be liberated from the cycle of birth and death.

तद्बुद्धयस्तदात्मानस्तन्निष्ठास्तत्परायणाः।
गच्छन्त्यपुनरावृत्तिं ज्ञाननिर्धूतकल्मषाः॥

Bhagavad Gita 5-17

"Those whose intellect is fixed in God, who are wholly absorbed in God, with firm faith in Him as the supreme goal, such persons quickly reach the state from which there is no return, their sins having been dispelled by the light of knowledge."

These three practices are not separate or independent of each other. They work together toward a common goal, that is the realization that the object world is non-different from the Self. These practices are different only in the manner in which they reinforce the subjective unity in all the perceived objects. According to Shankara, *shravaNa, manana, nididhyAsana* are three milestones on a single path. They all facilitate the same experience of the Self, but in varying proportions. Practicing them is like pounding the grain to separate the rice from the chaff. There is no limit on the number of times the grain is pounded. It is pounded until it is separated from the chaff. As we mature in our practice, our efforts gradually dissolve into Consciousness, and Consciousness alone remains. Such dissolution is possible only when the effects of *prArabdha* karma are exhausted. The three-fold practice removes the effects of *prArabdha* karma.

Another contention may be raised here. Two knives cannot fit into a single sheath at the same time. If the first knife to enter the sheath is karma, how can a second knife called Knowledge enter the sheath at the same time? For one to be present, the other must be absent. We know that karma is already present since we continue to experience its effect all our life. Our efforts to attain Self-Knowledge, on the other hand, are relatively new, so Self-Knowledge appears to be completely out of our reach. Since past karma is stronger than our efforts to gain Self-Knowledge, we have to intensify our efforts (practice). But is it possible to intensify our practice when karma is operating so strongly?

The Operating Field of Karma

Shankara offers a practical answer. Even though karma has a great impact on our lives, he says we should not assume that it holds us in its grip forever. The extent to which karma operates is limited. It operates only until it culminates into a situation or experience where we are forced to enjoy the results – joy or misery – of our past actions. We cannot avoid the situation, since it is the result of actions performed in a previous life. It is too late to correct these past actions now, so we have no choice but to accept the consequences. It is only until the point when we experience the consequences of our past actions that karma operates.

Karma stops operating once it delivers the results of past actions. It has no control over what follows. We consider ourselves doers (performer of actions) and enjoyers (experiencer of the results). We do not have any control over the results of our past actions, but we do have freedom in choosing the actions we perform now. *prArabdha* karma has no influence over the actions we perform in the present.

Since *prArabdha* karma accumulates over many lifetimes, it hardens into an instinct and becomes the cause for rebirth. Since it is already in motion, it is like an arrow in flight that cannot be withdrawn. It is bound to deliver the results, good or bad. The new karma we are creating, on the other hand, is different. Shankara says the karma we decide to perform now is like an arrow that is strung and is yet to be released from the bow. We have control over it – we can choose to either release it or not release it. If it is simply left to karma to make the decision, it might incite us to release the arrow. Past karmas transform into strong tendencies. When particular conditions arise, these tendencies manifest as strong likes and dislikes and propel us into taking corresponding actions. They manipulate our thought process and reduce our capacity to discriminate. We need to be alert to these tendencies, discriminate between right and wrong, perform appropriate actions, and refrain from others. As human beings, we certainly have the capacity to discriminate and act appropriately, and not blindly follow our tendencies.

Human Effort versus Destiny

This ability to introspect before taking any action is called *puruShakAram* or human effort. This is different from simply surrendering to past karma and leaving everything to fate. This debate is commonly referred to as the debate between destiny and free will. Some argue that everything is preordained by karma, while others argue that it is driven by human effort or lack of it. According to Shankara, both are extreme perspectives. Karma has an impact only on the results of our past actions and, at the best, can trigger tendencies, such as likes and dislikes. Beyond that, it has no impact on our ability to discriminate and take control of our actions. We have the capacity to discriminate, weigh-in on the pros and cons of performing actions, and take the appropriate actions. It is this ability to discriminate and act accordingly that empowers us. Since we can create new karma consciously, *prArabdha* karma has no impact on it. New effort and past results are mutually exclusive.

If this is not true, we would not be able to make any decisions or perform any actions in life. If everything is attributed to past karma, then the question we need to answer is, how did *prArabdha* karma accumulate in the first place? It accumulated because of the actions we performed in the past. Obviously, we had the freedom to perform those actions. How can this power to decide and freedom to act disappear suddenly now? We certainly continue to have the power to choose the actions we want to perform. We should leverage this power and perform appropriate actions. This is called *puruShaprayatnam*, human effort or free will. While *prArabdha* karma binds us on one hand, the new karma we generate can liberate us from bondage. While one is a problem, the other is a solution. The solution is hidden in the problem. A thorn is required to remove another thorn. Similarly, new effort is required to remove the residue of old karma. While past karma might take us deeper into the material world, the new karma we perform can take us deeper into the knowledge of the Self. This new karma is the practice of listening to the scripture (*shravaNa*), contemplating on its meaning (*manana*), and experiencing the Self by meditating on it with single-pointed concentration (*nididhyAsana*).

Purification of the Mind and Senses

"What is the guarantee that these practices will produce the desired results?" one may ask. Even after years of listening to the scripture, we may still not grasp its meaning. What is the use of human effort if it does not yield the desired results? Shankara has a practical answer for us. If we do not get the desired results in spite of our practice, Shankara says it is because of strong tendencies (*samskAra-s*) that are a residue of our past karma. These tendencies obstruct our progress and prevent us from attaining our goal. The Upanishad declares, "It is rare indeed to find someone who has had the direct experience of the Self and is capable of teaching another person. Equally rare it is to find someone who has grasped the essence of the teaching."

श्रवणायापि बहुभिर्यो न लभ्यः श्रृण्वन्तोऽपि बहवो यं न विद्युः।
आश्चर्यो वक्ता कुशलोऽस्य लब्धाऽऽश्चर्यो ज्ञाता कुशलानुशिष्टः॥

Katha Upanishad 1.2.7

"He (the self) of whom many are not even able to hear, whom many, even when they hear of him, do not comprehend; wonderful is a man, when found, who is able to teach the self; wonderful is he who comprehends the Self, when taught by an able teacher."

Hence, it is clear that it is possible to practice *shravaNa* and *manana* only if our tendencies allow us to do so. However, we should not be discouraged or intimidated by this. It is clearly not the intention of the scripture to intimidate us. Its intent is only to caution us about things that could hinder our progress and to encourage us to intensify our efforts. If we are not able to intensify our efforts in the three-fold practice, Shankara says, it might be because our mind and senses are not pure and refined. If that is the case, he suggests we cultivate the six-virtues (*shama, dama, uparati, titiksha, sraddha,* and *samAdhAna)* in order to gain control over our mind and develop tranquility. Since the three-fold practice (listening, reflecting, and experiencing the Self) is a practice in Self-enquiry, it is an internal practice. The six-fold practice, on the other hand, is external. Its goal is to take control of our senses and purify our minds. The sensory organs are referred to as instruments. It is only with the help of these instruments that we are able to perform all actions. They need to be pure in order to not obstruct our progress on the path to Self-Knowledge. Therefore, it is necessary to cultivate the six-virtues in order to purify our minds and make steady progress in the three-fold practice.

Some of our sense organs are internal and others are external. The internal organs are the mind (*manas*) and the life-force (*prANa*). The external organs that correspond to the mind are the five organs of knowledge, such as the sense of touch and taste. The external organs that correspond to the life-force are the organs of action, such as the hands, feet, and tongue. The organs of knowledge collect input from the external world, while the organs of action convey information externally. Mind-related organs help us to know, while the organs related to the life-force help us to act on what we know. Both mind and life-force are internal organs and need to be purified.

Once internal organs are purified, the external organs associated with them also get purified. The purification of these internal organs is called *shama* or tranquility. Purification of the mind leads to the purification of the life-force and vice versa. The effort to control external senses is called *dama*. If we master the virtues of *shama* and *dama*, we will have control over all our internal and external sense organs. Once we have control over our senses, we will be able to turn our attention away from the material world. This withdrawal from the worldly objects is called *uparati*. Even after withdrawing from the world, we may continue to confront polarities, such as likes and dislikes. We need to be patient and take a firm stance when we are confronted with conflicting emotions. Such patience is called *titiksha* or endurance. This is the fourth of the six-virtues. The fifth virtue is *sraddha* – intense faith and adherence to the teaching. *sraddha* leads to *samAdhi*, the complete abidance of the individual in the Self. This is the final step in the purification process.

Therefore, before we set forth on the path to Self-Knowledge, we must prepare for the journey. As Sage Vyasa said in the epic Mahabharata, we are all stained by past karma. We need to get rid of the stain before we start the process of self-inquiry. We can do so only after purifying our mind and sense organs by developing certain virtues. As the senses get purified, the power of karma weakens and transforms into a quest for knowledge. Efforts to listen, contemplate, and experience the truth will then progress smoothly.

Lord Yama provides similar instruction to Nachiketa in the Katha Upanishad.

नाविरतो दुश्चरितान्नाशान्तो नासमाहितः।
नाशान्तमानसो वाऽपि प्रज्ञानेनैनमाप्नुयात्॥

Katha Upanishad 1.2.24

"But he who has not turned away from bad conduct, whose senses are not subdued, whose mind is not concentrated, whose mind is not pacified, can never obtain this Atman by knowledge."

Those who perform actions that are condemned by the scripture, those who indulge in sensual pleasures, and those who are constantly distracted by desires cannot grasp the truth in spite of all their efforts.

Hence, to qualify for the practice of self-inquiry, *shravaNa, manana, and nididhyAsana*, we must purify our senses and mind. It is for this reason alone that the Upanishads describe rituals and methods of worship. Otherwise, there is no place for such dualistic practices in the Upanishads, which are an ocean of pure non-dual knowledge. These practices (rituals and worship) promote a sense of doer-ship since they require a doer, an action to be performed, and a result to be enjoyed. They do not promote the experience of the non-dual Self. They are like two oceans that are flowing in opposite directions. What is the use of swimming in the ocean on the east if the intent is to go west? Not only will we not reach our destination, but we will end up in a place that is completely contrary to our goal! Similarly, if we keep performing dualistic practices (rituals and worship), we will not only distance ourselves from the non-dual Self, but we will also get submerged in the not-Self (the object world).

Purification Through Karma

The Upanishads, therefore, describe worship and rituals only to purify our minds and senses and prepare us for Self-enquiry. Those who aspire for liberation must renounce not only the actions condemned by the scripture but also actions that are spurred by desire. As long as the mind is attached to pleasures now and hereafter (after death), it will have no peace. A restless mind is not conducive to Self-enquiry. Desires cause the mind to be restless, so they need to be eliminated. Once we give up all actions that are condemned by the scripture and driven by desires, we will be left with *nitya* karma or obligatory actions, such as learning and teaching, and *naimittika* karma or rituals performed on special occasions, such as childbirth and the death of a parent. Even such actions must not be performed for any worldly or heavenly pleasures, but with a desire for liberation. Materialists perform *nitya* and *naimittika* karma with ego and attachment. They think they alone are qualified to perform such actions and believe such actions will bring them great merit. Actions performed with such an attitude are sullied and will not produce the desired results. When true seekers of Self-Knowledge perform *nitya* and *naimittika* karma, they do so without any ego or attachment (me and mine). Since their actions remain unsullied, they produce the desired result, which is the purification of the mind and senses.

According to the scripture, when the individual who strives for Self-Knowledge performs rituals and worship, it is only to cleanse the body and senses. All actions are performed as an offering to the

Self. Not only the Vedas, which are of divine origin, but also other scriptures confirm this truth.

Krishna in Bhagavad Gita says,

यज्ञदानतप:कर्म न त्याज्यं कार्यमेव तत्।
यज्ञो दानं तपश्चैव पावनानि मनीषिणाम्॥

Bhagavad Gita, Ch 18-5

"Actions based upon sacrifice, charity, and penance should never be abandoned; they must certainly be performed. Indeed, acts of sacrifice, charity, and penance are purifying even for those who are wise."

Rituals and worship must be performed only for the purification of the mind and not to attain worldly or heavenly pleasures. According to the Upanishads, *nitya and naimittika* karmas purify our minds, while rituals and worship help us develop concentration. Shankara says it is possible to purify the mind through karma if all actions are performed as an offering to that which creates and sustains this entire universe. Only then will such actions result in the purification of the mind, which is a pre-requisite for attaining the Knowledge of the Self.

While the Upanishads suggest we perform all actions prescribed by the scripture with this attitude, Bhagavad Gita suggests we extend this attitude to every action we perform; even spontaneous bodily functions and worldly actions must be considered as an offering to the Lord.

कर्मण्यकर्म यः पश्येदकर्मणि च कर्म यः।
स बुद्धिमान्मनुष्येषु स युक्तः कृत्स्नकर्मकृत्॥
Bhagavad Gita - Ch 4-18॥

"Those who see action in inaction and inaction in action are truly wise amongst humans. Although performing all kinds of actions, they are yogis and masters of all their actions."

In every action we perform, we must be aware of the unmoving Consciousness that permeates every action.

नैव किञ्चित्करोमीति युक्तो मन्येत तत्ववित्।
पश्यञ्शृण्वन्स्पृशञ्जिघ्रन्नश्नन्गच्छन्स्वपञ्श्वसन्॥
Bhagavad Gita - Ch 5-8॥

प्रलपन्विसृजन्गृह्णन्नुन्मिषन्निमिषन्नपि।
इन्द्रियाणीन्द्रियार्थेषु वर्तन्त इति धारयन्॥ -
Bhagavad Gita - Ch 5-9॥

"Those steadfast in this *karm yog* always think 'I am not the doer,' even while engaged in seeing, hearing, touching, smelling, moving, sleeping, breathing, speaking, excreting, and grasping, and opening or closing the eyes. With the light of divine knowledge, they see that it is only the material senses that are moving amongst their objects."

All bodily actions – seeing, hearing, breathing, eliminating – must be attributed to the Absolute Consciousness. Only when all actions are performed as an offering to the Absolute, they produce results that benefit us, and not just the obvious pleasure and pain.

Sri Krishna in Bhagavad Gita called this karma yoga – union with the Lord through action. Rituals and worship by themselves are not karma yoga. They must be performed as an offering to the Lord. Without such an attitude, our ego and attachment will continue. For as long as ego and attachment exist, the mind cannot be pure. Karma yoga is the only tool that can purify the mind. When the mind is purified, the Knowledge of the Self arises. When we start seeing that all actions are appearing in Consciousness, we start renouncing them (doer-ship). When the Knowledge of the Self matures, we experience the Self as Pure Consciousness. By attributing all actions to Consciousness, we stop seeing duality. We, therefore, benefit in two ways by practicing karma yoga. We attain tranquility of mind (*shama*) and control over senses (*dama*), which in turn will reduce the impact of past karma (*prArabdha*). We will cultivate a pure mind that will be capable of listening and contemplating on the great teachings of the scripture.

Most worshipers blindly perform rituals without understanding this truth. They think it is enough to just worship a deity and perform the rituals described by the scripture. Not only do they believe this, but they also force others to believe this and condemn those who do not. This is unwarranted. These are mere ritualists and not karma yogis. Only when an action (karma) unites the individual with the creator, it is karma yoga. That is true religion. In Bhagavad Gita, Krishna declared that karma yoga is His religion, and those who ignore it will be lost forever!

ये मे मतमिदं नित्यमनुतिष्ठन्ति मानवा:।
श्रद्धावन्तोऽनसूयन्तो मुच्यन्ते तेऽपि कर्मभि:॥
Bhagavad Gita 3-31॥

'Those who abide by these teachings of mine, with profound faith and free from cavil, are released from the bondage of karma."

मयि सर्वाणि कर्माणि संन्यस्याध्यात्मचेतसा।
निराशीर्निनर्ममो भूत्वा युध्यस्व विगतज्वर:॥
Bhagavad Gita 3-30॥

"Performing all works as an offering unto me, constantly meditate on me as the Supreme. Become free from desire and selfishness, and with your mental grief departed, fight!"

All actions, including worldly actions and those prescribed by the scripture, must be performed with discrimination, without ego or attachment, and must be attributed to the Supreme Self. This then becomes karma yoga and not ritualism.

यामिमां पुष्पितां वाचं प्रवदन्त्यविपश्चित:।
वेदवादरता: पार्थ नान्यदस्तीति वादिन:॥
कामात्मान: स्वर्गपरा जन्मकर्मफलप्रदाम्।
क्रियाविशेषबहुलां भोगैश्वर्यगतिं प्रति॥
Bhagavad Gita 2-42-43

"Those with limited understanding get attracted to the flowery words of the Vedas, which advocate ostentatious rituals for elevation to the celestial abodes, and presume no higher principle is described in them. They glorify only those portions of the Vedas that please their senses, and perform pompous ritualistic ceremonies for attaining high birth, opulence, sensual enjoyment, and elevation to the heavenly planets."

If ritualism is not a true religion, are rituals then useless? Shankara says rituals are useless in the realization of the Self if they are performed with ego and not with an attitude of karma yoga.

The Yoga of Action and Knowledge

Earlier we stated that Knowledge is the only means for attaining the Supreme Self. But now we are stating karma yoga as an essential practice. Isn't karma yoga also karma? By accepting karma as a means for Self-realization, aren't we contradicting the fundamental principle of Advaita? Shankara says neither external karma yoga practices like *shama* and *dama* nor internal practices like *shravaNa* and *manana* will lead directly to Self-realization. They only help in removing the effects of past karma and ignorance about our true nature. This is a step-by-step process. As a first step, the effects of past karma are removed by performing positive actions. As a second step, through the practice of karma yoga, tranquility of the mind, control over the senses, and detachment are cultivated. When the mind is purified, internal practices like *shravaNa* and *manana* can be easily intensified. As a result of all these practices, the knowledge of the Self as Pure Consciousness will arise automatically. Since Consciousness is already present, these practices do not create anything new. They simply help us get in touch with what is already present as our essential nature.

While *shama* and *dama* take us a few steps closer to Consciousness, *shravaNa* and *manana* take us several more steps closer to it.

Karma yoga with its *shama* and *dama* practices is considered a religion, while *jnAna* yoga with its *shravaNa* and *manana* practices is considered a philosophy. If we practice both karma and *jnAna* yoga seriously, we gradually decrease the effects of *prArabdha* karma. While reducing the effects of past karma, we improve our understanding and Knowledge of the Self. Nature provides ample opportunity for this process to happen. Recognizing this truth, we must march resolutely toward our goal and not surrender helplessly to destiny. Helplessness is nothing but laziness. The principle of karma is not expected to make us lazy. We cannot undo the past, but the future is in our hands. Karma yoga instructs us to perform good actions now and break the cycle of past bad karma. The scripture alerts us to this truth.

उत्तिष्ठत जाग्रत प्राप्य वरान्निबोधत।
क्षुरस्य धारा निशिता दुरत्यया दुर्गं पथस्तत्कवयो वदन्ति
Katha Upanishad 1.3.14

"Arise, awake; having reached the great, learn; the edge of a razor is sharp and impassable; that path, the intelligent say, is hard to go by."

In spite of such strong encouragement from the scripture and the sages, we continue to be plagued by doubts. We wonder if it is possible for ordinary people like us, who are caught up in worldly life, to practice Self-enquiry. Even if we practice, we ask – will we get the results we are seeking? Such thoughts are discouraging. Scripture does not tolerate such a pessimistic attitude.

Sri Krishna says in Bhagavad Gita that a doubting mind will lead to one's downfall.

अज्ञश्चाश्रद्दधानश्च संशयात्मा विनश्यति।
नायं लोकोऽस्ति न परो न सुखं संशयात्मनः॥

Bhagavad Gita 4-40

"But persons who possess neither faith nor knowledge, and who are of a doubting nature, suffer a downfall. For the skeptical souls, there is no happiness either in this world or the next."

We can experience the Self just like we experience the objects we perceive, and the method for experiencing the Self is also quite simple.

राजविद्या राजगुह्यं पवित्रमिदमुत्तमम्।
प्रत्यक्षावगमं धर्म्यं सुसुखं कर्तुमव्ययम्॥

Bhagavad Gita 9-2

"This knowledge is the king of sciences and the most profound of all secrets. It purifies those who hear it. It is directly realizable, in accordance with *dharma*, easy to practice, and everlasting in effect."

Shankara says we continue to be plagued by doubts because we lack a good teacher and a passion for the teaching. When there is no teacher or interest in the teaching, the mind constantly seeks worldly matters and puts no effort to acquire Self-Knowledge. Although Consciousness is the very nature of our Self, It will continue to be out of our reach, and we will experience only the not-Self (world). However, Shankara says, those who are blessed with a teacher and whose minds are turned inwards toward the Self are bound to experience the bliss of the Self.

Therefore, there is no doubt that even average people like us have the capacity to attain Self-Knowledge. Consciousness pervades everything equally, from the ant to the creator Brahma. Recognizing this for a fact, gods and sages persevered in their practice and acquired many profound insights. Sage Vamadeva, for instance, even while he was in his mother's womb, declared that he is everything, the sun, moon, and stars! Shankara says Vamadeva could say so with such confidence only because of the power he had attained from meditating on the non-dual mantra "I am *brahman*." Since Consciousness is our very own nature, it is quite possible to experience It. We just need to own It and strive to experience It.

यत्नाद्यतमानस्तु योगी संशुद्धकिल्बिष:।
अनेकजन्मसंसिद्धस्ततो याति परां गतिम्॥
Bhagavad Gita 6-45॥

"With the accumulated merits of many past births, when these yogis engage in sincere endeavor in making further progress, they become purified from material desires and attain perfection in this life itself."

बहूनां जन्मनामन्ते ज्ञानवान्मां प्रपद्यते।
वासुदेव: सर्वमिति स महात्मा सुदुर्लभ:॥
Bhagavad Gita 7-19॥

"After many births of spiritual practice, one who is endowed with knowledge surrenders unto me, knowing me to be all that is. Such a great soul is indeed very rare."

As we continue our practice in every birth, we will gradually accumulate the wealth of Self-Knowledge, and eventually, in one final birth, we will attain full realization of the Self.

Competency

Just because we said effort and practice are necessary, we cannot assume that everyone is required or capable of practicing all the *sAdhana*-s all their lives – karma yoga, *samAdhi* yoga, *shravaNa,* and *manana.* It is the capacity of the individual that determines which practice is right for him or her. Our spiritual journey did not begin in this very birth. It must have started several lifetimes ago and will potentially continue for several more in the future. For some, this current birth might be in the middle of the cycle, and for others, it might be the end of the cycle. Therefore, the particular practices we undertake depends on our competency and maturity. Rituals may appeal to the average student, while karma yoga might appeal to a more mature one. Those who yearn for knowledge might gravitate toward *shravaNa* and *manana,* and once they attain maturity in their understanding, they will want to practice *nididhyAsana,* which is the ultimate practice.

ये यथा मां प्रपद्यन्ते तांस्तथैव भजाम्यहम्।
मम वर्त्मानुवर्तन्ते मनुष्या: पार्थ सर्वश:॥
Bhagavad Gita 4-11

"In whatever way people surrender unto me, I reciprocate with them accordingly. Everyone follows my path, knowingly or unknowingly, O Partha."

In his commentary on the above verse, Shankara says the Lord bestows Knowledge on those who aspire for Knowledge and have developed dispassion, liberation on those who have attained Self-Knowledge, and freedom from misery on those who pray to be free of suffering.

In this manner, the practice (*sAdhana*) that is appropriate to us corresponds to our competency, and the results we attain from our practice correspond to the effort we put into our practice.

Benefits of the Various Practices

There is no single solution for all problems. Some might perform rituals, while others might practice karma yoga. Some might strive for *shama* and *dama*, while others may be concentrating on *shravaNa* and *manana*.

It is foolish to assume that we must continue to perform all rituals and worship until we mature in Self-Knowledge and develop dispassion. Rituals are not the noblest of actions. Karma yoga is nobler than performing rituals, and *shravaNa* and *manana* are far nobler than karma yoga. Reading and reflecting on the Upanishads is a much more valuable activity than performing rituals. The point is not about performing or not performing rituals. It is about the purification of the mind and intellect. If a person who does not have a pure mind performs rituals, the rituals will remain as spurious actions and will not yield the expected results. A person who has a pure mind and the ability to discriminate could freely choose to perform or not perform rituals.

यस्त्वात्मरतिरेव स्यादात्मतृप्तश्च मानव:।
आत्मन्येव च सन्तुष्टस्तस्य कार्यं न विद्यते॥
Bhagavad Gita 3-17॥

"But those who rejoice in the Self, who are illumined and fully satisfied in the Self, for them, there is no duty."

Meditation on the nature of the Self is *dhyAna*. One-pointed concentration and union with the Self is Yoga. These are the only two tasks seekers of Self-Knowledge need to perform. There is no need for them to chant mantras or perform rituals.

It is sheer foolishness if we continue to perform rituals in spite of the scripture clearly assuring us that seekers of Self-Knowledge are not required to perform any rituals. We would be just as guilty as the ones who blindly perform rituals without any interest in Self-Knowledge. We cannot compare the two. There is no connection between performing rituals and Self-enquiry. One thing does not aid the other. If we don't realize this truth, we will be deceiving ourselves. We want to be perceived as non-dualists, but in reality, we do not have the commitment and maturity of the mind to practice non-duality. Instead, we waste time performing actions that are not conducive to Self-Knowledge.

We cannot find fault with the ritualists or the worshipers. A squint-eye is better than a blind-eye! Even if ritualists are not interested in

Self-Knowledge, they are at least performing righteous actions with a dutiful attitude. This is better than living a careless life, performing sinful actions. Righteous actions give satisfaction and faith in the existence of God. Gradually, this faith will lead to karma yoga and, eventually, to an interest in listening to the non-dual teachings of the scripture. Instead of living a materialistic life with no clear purpose, it is better to respect and follow the traditions of the elders. Instead of living like an animal driven by instinct, it is better to live with a sense of duty and righteousness. As long as we are walking on the right path, we will eventually reach our goal. Shankara says this is the essence of the scripture.

Compassion

We cannot know how many lives a person has lived in the past, but we can deduce the type of a person he or she is by his or her behavior and tendencies. Their external behaviors indicate their internal tendencies. If a person does not show any interest in performing worship and rituals, that person may have matured into a karma yogi. If a person is always reading scriptures, contemplating on the teaching, and discussing with like-minded people, that person may have transcended karma yoga and is now seeking Self-Knowledge. If a person is not interested in discussions but spends his time in silent Self-enquiry, that person may have matured in Self-Knowledge. Individuals who have developed dispassion and matured in Self-Knowledge might completely renounce the material world. People become renunciates for different reasons. Some become renunciates with the desire to read and reflect on the great non-dual teachings of the scripture in seclusion. Others may only want to spend their time in continuous abidance in the Self. Shankara says that such people do not need any external symbols of renunciation, such as the ochre robes or the staff of the traditional renunciate (*sanyAsa*).

People have different levels of competencies. Ritualists must understand that rituals are only the first step in the journey and not a destination by themselves. Seekers of Self-Knowledge should not dismiss rituals and worship as mere superstitions. Such mutual respect and understanding of each other will develop equanimity and compassion for others.

A student does not wish to remain as a student forever. Her aim is to become as good as the teacher, so she does not expect the teacher to come down to her level. Just because the teacher is at a higher level, the teacher does not look down on the student with contempt. He does not forget that he was also a student at one time. He may not mingle with his students, but he will accept their strengths and weaknesses and help them become as competent as himself. Only then will the teacher-student relationship benefit each other. Ritualists and Knowledge-seekers must have a similar relationship. They would then be traveling on paths that are intertwined, rather than paths that are completely diverse.

Once we are on the right path, we must stay focused and continue our practice with a one-track mind for the rest of our lives. As we mature in our practice and attain higher levels of knowledge, our *prArabdha* karma loses its intensity. When *prArabdha* karma weakens and our practice intensifies, we will attain Self-Knowledge.

Need for a Guru

Do we need a guru to lead us in our practice? Shankara insisted many times in all his commentaries that both the scripture and the teacher are essential. In his commentary on the Prasna Upanishad, Shankar declared that one can transcend the phenomenal world and attain the Absolute Knowledge of the Self only with the help of a teacher. In his commentary on Mundaka Upanishad, he stated that bookish knowledge will transform into experience only when that knowledge is transmitted by an eminent teacher. Chandogya Upanishad declared that the one who has a teacher will certainly know the way.

Every teaching has subtleties that cannot be easily comprehended. We need an expert who is capable of understanding all the intricacies to teach us. There might be an abundance of medical knowledge freely available, but we need an expert medical professional to teach it. There might be plenty of law books, but we need an expert lawyer to interpret the laws and argue on our behalf in the court. If it is important to have an experienced teacher to teach worldly subjects, it is even more important to have an enlightened teacher to guide us in attaining the Supreme Knowledge of the Self.

The teacher or the guru does not have to be a living person, as long as that person is amply equipped with Self-Knowledge. Just because we need a teacher, we should not pick any dummy figure for a teacher without discrimination. Such teachers will only become a burden on us. Shankara says, such teachers, being ignorant themselves, will lead their followers also into ignorance.

We would be most fortunate if we can find eminent teachers like Sage Suka or Sage Yagnyavalkya. If we cannot find such eminent teachers, instead of ending up with mediocre ones, it is better to rely on the scripture. Whatever we choose, teacher or the scripture, Shankara says, we need to make sure they are an authentic source of knowledge. Whoever assumes the role of the teacher, if they are providing us with the knowledge of the Self, they should be regarded as our teacher. There is a story in Brihadaranyaka Upanishad that illustrates this point. In the beginning, when the world was first created, Lord Brahma, the creator, looked around and, finding himself all alone, was scared. He recovered from his fear within a few moments and asked himself, "When there is no one other than my Self, what is there for me to be afraid of?" The knowledge that the Self alone exists removed all fears!

Commenting on this story, Shankara fires off several questions: How did Lord Brahma get the vision of non-duality? Who taught him the knowledge of the Self? Did he have a guru? If Brahma could attain Self-Knowledge without the help of a guru, it is possible for anyone to do so as well. Deep yearning for the truth and one-pointed concentration, combined with *shravaNa, manana,* and *nididhyAsana,* are invariably the most effective means for attaining Self-Knowledge. If one has completed these practices in previous lifetimes and has accrued the merits of such practices, it is possible for that person to attain Self-Knowledge in this very life without the aid of a guru. If one has not performed any such practices in previous lifetimes, a guru is absolutely essential. Therefore, it is the results of past *sAdhana* that determine whether or not a guru is necessary in this life.

We should not rush to find a teacher and inadvertently pick the wrong one. Instead, we should study the scripture, the ultimate source of knowledge, and contemplate on its teachings. If we are not capable of doing so, we should cultivate virtues, such as *shama* and *dama*, or perform all actions as an offering to the Lord (karma yoga). This will purify our body and mind, sharpen our intellect, and improve our ability to discriminate. As our practice matures and our discriminatory power increases, the results of past actions start diminishing and we find ourselves continuously contemplating on the Self. Deep contemplation on the Self is in itself the experience of the Self. When we say knowledge is experience, we are not referring to simply knowing the meaning of the words we hear, but rather an in-depth and experiential understanding of the Self that leaves a deep impression in our minds. These deep impressions help us discriminate and separate the Self from the not-Self, the substratum from the superimposition (object world). This is not an easy process. It requires immense vigilance and perseverance. But this is the only effort that is required. If we persist in our efforts, *prArabdha* karma will slowly dissipate, and our efforts will start yielding the expected results. According to Shankara, we may experience the results in this life or in a subsequent life depending on the intensity of our current efforts and the power of past karma. We should not, however, be discouraged by this. If we continue our practice with discrimination and dispassion, the practice itself will remove all hurdles from our path. Shankara assures us that relentless practice will certainly take us to our ultimate goal – the experience of the Self as Pure Infinite Consciousness.

Conclusion

Following are some conclusions we can draw from the above discussion. Consciousness is the very nature of our Self, so we are already free of bondage. Due to primordial ignorance, we forgot our essential nature several lifetimes ago and succumbed to *samsAra*. To remind us of our essential nature, the scripture equips us with the knowledge of the Self. As we contemplate the nature of the Self, ignorance is dispelled. Our minds assume the form of Consciousness, and we experience our Self as Consciousness. Since results of past actions (karma) obstruct and delay our progress, we must make additional efforts to get rid of them and purify our minds. Depending on how pure and refined our minds are, we must practice *shama* and *dama* or *shravaNa, manana,* and *nididhyAsana.* The first set of practices lead to the second set of practices. When we mature in the second set of practices, we will start experiencing the results. In the non-dual path, not every person requires a guru. Whatever or whoever aids the seeker in experiencing the Self – the scripture or the teacher – is a guru. Sincere practice will eventually culminate in the experience of the Self. Such an experience can occur in this very life or in a subsequent life. We must be patient and not compromise on our practice. If we continue to doubt and question our ability, we will lose all motivation to practice. Therefore, with unflinching fidelity to truth, if we continue our efforts with commitment and resolution, we will certainly attain our goal.

Liberation

In the previous chapter, we discussed how virtues like *shama* and *dama* purify our mind and intensify our efforts in Self-inquiry. We also discussed how Self-inquiry eventually culminates in the experiential Knowledge of the Self. In this chapter, we will discuss the benefits of Self-inquiry and the experience of the Self. No one, not even a foolish person, will want to do anything unless there is a benefit associated with it. For us to be motivated to cultivate these virtues and remain committed to Self-inquiry (*Advaita sAdhana*), we must be assured of a significant benefit in doing so.

Liberation (*mukti*)

According to Shankara, freedom from suffering and the cycle of birth and death (*samsAra*) is the goal and benefit of all non-dual practices and the ultimate experience of the Self. This freedom from *samsAra* is called liberation (*mukti*). Both *mukti* and *mOksha* mean emancipation. To be liberated from *samsAra*, one needs to give up attachment to the object world. Non-dual disciplines help us develop detachment, which in turn leads to freedom from *samsAra*.

Is escape from misery (*samsAra*) the only benefit we derive from *mOksha*? Isn't *samsAra* unreal? If so, how can escape from something unreal be a benefit? Shouldn't we gain something more substantial from Self-realization?

Shankara agrees that *mukti* is not a mere escape from the misery of *samsAra* but has a more distinct and tangible benefit. *mukti* is not like a fruit that one can simply reach out and pluck. It is also not located in some distant place somewhere. Neither is it something that someone can hand over to us in a platter. Most people, including scholars, have wrong notions about liberation and the process of attaining it. Not only are they misled by such wrong notions, but they also mislead others! They encourage others to perform rituals and worship with the promise that such actions will take them to other worlds, where their favorite deities will graciously bestow upon them *mukti*!

The Nature of Liberation

Shankara says that people make such claims because their minds are conditioned by time, space, and causality. Liberation, *mukti*, is not available in some distant location or time. If it is available only in a particular location and time, it implies that it is not available in the current location and time. *mukti* is not like the worldly objects we perceive with our senses. *mukti* is beyond time and space. It does not have a name or a form. It is just being *brahman*, Pure Consciousness, which is the very nature of our Self. Due to beginning-less ignorance (lack of Knowledge of the Self), the Self has receded to the background and the not-Self (object world) has come into the foreground. When the Knowledge of the Self arises in us, our natural state of being *brahman* returns to the foreground, and we slowly start experiencing It. It is like the return of good health after a bout of sickness.

mukti is the natural state of the Self. It has no beginning or an end. If it appears suddenly, then it would disappear just as suddenly. Such liberation is of no use to anyone. Shankara cautions us against such thoughts since they take us back into *samsAra*.

We must examine and understand the significance of the term *mukti* thoroughly before we make any assumptions based on the stories we hear from mythology. *mukti* is an experience that is unlike the experience of any object in the material world. In the material world, the subject (experiencer) is different from the object that is experienced. In *mukti*, there is no such difference between the subject and the object because there is no scope for anything other than the subject to exist. *mukti* is the experience of the subject, which is one's own Self. Can Self experience Itself? Can fire burn itself? Shankara says fire is inert, so it cannot burn itself. But Self is Pure Consciousness. Since awareness is Its very nature, the Self can become aware of Itself, just as It is aware of the objects of the world. The Self can become aware of Itself when the objects of the world lose their separate existence. Self (Consciousness) does not depend on the object world for Its existence. Self is the "I AM" awareness that is eternally present, regardless of the presence or absence of objects.

That "beingness" itself is called *mukti*. Since It is pure awareness with no "other," there is no suffering. Since It is the feeling that "I alone AM," there is only happiness. It is a state of being where misery is naturally absent, and happiness alone is present. Since It is not connected with the body, mind, or other adjuncts, It is free and unrestricted. Since It is not out there somewhere but right here as our awareness, It is our very nature. Since It is our very nature, It is ever-present. Liberation or *mukti*, therefore, is the identity with the Absolute, Unchanging Reality that is the Self. According to Shankara, Self, Knowledge of the Self, and Liberation are not three different things. Self is the same as the Knowledge of the Self, and Knowledge of the Self is the same as Liberation.

Types of Liberation

According to Shankara, *mukti* is of two types – *jIvanmukti* and *videhamukti*. *jIvanmukti* is the experience of liberation while the body is still alive, and *videhamukti* is the experience of liberation after the body dies. No religion or advocate of a religion would accept this. They would argue that liberation is possible only after the death of the body, and not before that. Only staunch Advaitins like Shankara, who have had direct experience of the Self, can declare with conviction that liberation (*mukti*) is certainly possible when the body is still alive.

A contention may be raised here. If Self is non-dual, the experience of liberation must also be non-dual. Why do we then differentiate between the experience of the *jIvanmukta* and the *videhamukta*?

This is a valid question. We must note, however, that the differentiation made between the two is not based on the nature of liberation itself, but rather on the timing when it occurs. Shankara says liberation is possible at any time as soon as all the necessary conditions are met. This could happen when the body is alive or after its death. If it happens when the body is still alive, it is called *Jīvanmukti*. If it happens after the body dies, it is called *videhamukti*.

Jivanmukti

If *mukti* is a state of Pure Consciousness with no identification with the body or mind, how can a person be liberated if the person's body and mind continue to exist? Shankara says no identification with the body does not mean that the perception of the body stops altogether. It simply means that identification with the body as "me" or "mine" stops. From the standpoint of the Self, which is the Absolute Reality, the body is just an illusion. Only because of our identification with the body, we believe it is real. From a metaphorical standpoint, dualists maintain that the body is real. In a metaphorical comparison, two different things are personified as each other because they share some common attributes. For instance, we may say that a young boy is a lion even though the lion and the boy are two separate things. Because the boy demonstrates some characteristics of a lion, such as fearlessness, we attribute the qualities of the lion to the boy and call him a lion. We make such an attribution knowing fully well that the two are different. On the other hand, if we mistake a pillar for a thief in the dark and scream for help in fear, it is only because we lack the knowledge of the pillar. This misapprehension of the real nature of an entity is illusion.

The body is an illusory manifestation. Consciousness is the only substance that is real and ever-present. There is no other separate entity. Just as a pillar is mistaken for a thief because of the lack of knowledge of the pillar, the body is mistaken to be real because of the lack of knowledge of the Self. Ritualists assume the body is real only because of their attachment to the body. The moment attachment to an object drops, the object also drops. Just as the illusion of the thief ceases as soon as the knowledge of the pillar arises, identification with the body ceases when identification with the Self arises. The body of the *jīvanmukta* will continue to appear as a separate entity to others, but the *jīvanmukta* perceives his body only as a shadow of Consciousness. Hence, the existence of the body is not an obstacle to liberation. If the existence of a body itself is bondage, then we would have to agree that all Self-realized beings who are alive on earth today are in bondage, while all ordinary beings who are dead are liberated! This is not a logical or a fair statement. Hence, it is not the existence of the body, but the identification with the body that leads to bondage. Therefore, it is certainly possible to be liberated even while the body is still alive.

Immediate and Experiential Results

People who worship the divine in particular forms do not experience the Self directly. They follow a step-by-step and gradual process called *krama-mukti*. After death, such people go to Satyaloka, where they are provided the knowledge of the Self. Only after they complete the training and experience the Self, they attain liberation.

Unlike the *krama-mukta*-s, the *jīvanmukta*-s are immediately liberated upon death due to their perfect knowledge and direct experience of the Self. Liberation is an immediate and experiential result of non-dual "realization." The moment we get a glimpse of our true nature (Self-Knowledge), we get a taste of liberation. Unlike rituals and worship, Knowledge does not involve any action. It is reflective in nature. Hence, the result (*mukti*) it yields is immediate. Liberation is the very nature of the Self. Self is Pure Consciousness that permeates everything. It is ever-present. When Self alone Is and *mukti* is the very nature of the Self, then it is possible to experience liberation even when the body is still alive.

If liberation is possible only after death, there would be no living person on the earth with Self-Knowledge! If this is true, there would be no one who could teach the rest of us the Knowledge of the Self. However, the Upanishad clearly instructs us to acquire the Knowledge of the Self from an eminent teacher (guru).

An eminent teacher is one who has grasped the Self *as is* and abides in the Self every moment of his life. Such a person is *brahman* (Consciousness) Itself and is free of all identification with the body and mind. Just because he continues to have a body, the *jIvanmukta* is not in bondage like the rest of us who are identified with the body. We cannot dismiss his knowledge as mere bookish knowledge. Knowledge of the Self is not worth much if it cannot be actualized into experience. A teacher must have direct experience before he or she can teach students. If everyone, including the teacher, is in bondage, then what is the meaning of liberation? If liberation is not possible while still alive, what is the guarantee that it is possible after death? According to Shankara, a formless substance (Self) can be comprehended only with the help of a form (teacher). If it is not possible for a living teacher to be Self-realized and liberated, it would also not be possible for a student to acquire knowledge and develop an intellect that can grasp the nature of the Self. The teacher-student relationship would become meaningless. In the teacher-student tradition, the teacher does not merely pass on his scriptural knowledge to the student; what he teaches arises from his own immediate experiential Knowledge of the Self.

Self is already present and does not have to be newly acquired. The moment ignorance is removed, the Self is revealed. The moment Self is revealed, Self is experienced. No particular action is required once Self is experienced. Liberation is the appearance of Self-Knowledge and disappearance of ignorance. Arising of Knowledge and removal of ignorance can happen only when the body and mind are alive and functioning. Therefore, body and mind cannot be an impediment to liberation (*mukti*).

The Body of the Jivanmukta

Even if we accept that liberation is possible in this very lifetime, we continue to be plagued with doubts. If all adjuncts (body and mind) are expected to dissolve into the Self when one attains liberation, how can the *jIvanmukta* be liberated if he continues to have a body? Isn't the body a bondage? Shankara says the body is not a bondage. Of the three types of karma, *sancita* (past) and *AgAmi* (new) karmas totally dissipate when the knowledge of the Self arises. Since all accrued karma is dissipated and no new karma is created, the *jīvanmukta* is no longer subject to rebirth. The current body will continue to exist, since it is the result of *prArabdha* karma that is already in motion. It is like an arrow in flight that cannot be withdrawn. Nothing can stop its momentum. It is bound to deliver the results, good or bad. Like the arrow that falls upon hitting the target, *prArabdha* karma ceases to exist soon after it produces the results of past actions. Like a potter's wheel that continues to spin as long as there is momentum, the body of the *jīvanmukta* continues to live as long as *prArabdha* karma continues to operate. The body came into existence because of *prArabdha* and ceases to exist when *prArabdha* is exhausted. According to the Upanishad, the body typically does not remain alive for long once a person attains the Knowledge of the Self. When the body ceases to exist, the effulgent Self alone remains.

Detachment

Therefore, the body is not an impediment to *mukti*. It is the identification and attachment to the body that is the impediment. It is hard not to identify with the body when we continue to experience thirst, hunger, and other pains and pleasures associated with the body. Although the body itself does not experience anything, since it is inert, the sentient mind does. If the *jīvanmukta* also continues to experience all the problems associated with the body, how can he continue to be liberated?

Even though the body is alive, the *jīvanmukta* is not attached to it. Therefore, he does not identify with the pains and pleasures associated with the body. He remains a witness to the body and to every experience associated with it. He dissolves everything into the Self and perceives everything, including his body and experiences of the body, as Self only. This is very different from the dualistic experience of an ordinary person who has a subject-object relationship with the world. For the *jīvanmukta*, there is only the Self (subject) and no object separate from the Self. He perceives everything as Self, which means that he experiences everything as undifferentiated Consciousness. His experience is not dualistic. In such an undifferentiated non-dual experience of the Self, there is no joy or sorrow. When the entire world, with its sentient and insentient parts, dissolves into the Self and Self alone IS, there is no room for anything other than the Self. While others continue to see his body as a separate object, the *jīvanmukta* sees all objects, including his body, as Pure Consciousness.

It is possible to experience such undifferentiated Consciousness while the body is still alive! Shankara says, not only the scripture, even our own experience proves it. The scripture (teaching) must correspond to the experience of the individual for it to be considered an authentic source of knowledge (*pramāNa*). Shankara describes the state of the *jīvanmukta* beautifully in his commentary: "While eating, resting, and performing other tasks, the *jīvanmukta* does not consider himself the doer. He attributes all his actions to his sense organs, which he knows are made up of the three *guNa*-s (*sattva, rajas,* and *tamas*) that interact with the corresponding three *guNa*-s of the world. Fully aware of this every moment of his life, the *jīvanmukta* does not take any ownership or doer-ship for the activities his body performs."

According to the scripture, actions performed with such a detached attitude do not generate any karmic effects or new karma because the effects of such actions are completely burned in the fire of Self-Knowledge. There have been many sages in the past and there will be many more in the future who experience such profound states of Consciousness. Krishna's words in the Bhagavad Gita clearly illustrate this.

त्यक्त्वा कर्मफलासङ्गं नित्यतृप्तो निराश्रयः।
कर्मण्यभिप्रवृत्तोऽपि नैव किञ्चित्करोति सः॥
Bhagavad Gita 4:20॥

"Such people, having given up attachment to the fruits of their actions, are always satisfied and not dependent on external things. Despite engaging in activities, they do not do anything at all."

अनादित्वान्निर्गुणत्वात्परमात्मायमव्ययः।
शरीरस्थोऽपि कौन्तेय न करोति न लिप्यते॥
Bhagavad Gita 13:32॥

"The Supreme Self is imperishable, without beginning, and devoid of any material qualities, O son of Kunti. Although situated within the body, It neither acts nor is It tainted by material energy."

सर्वकर्माणि मनसा संन्यस्यास्ते सुखं वशी।
नवद्वारे पुरे देही नैव कुर्वन्न कारयन्॥
Bhagavad Gita 5:13:॥

"The embodied beings who are self-controlled and detached reside happily in the city of nine gates, free from thinking they are the doers or the cause of anything."

Thus, even though the *jīvanmukta* has a body and performs actions, his actions do not generate karma or results of any kind. Unlike ordinary individuals who are totally identified with the body as "me," the *jīvanmukta* considers his body only as a temporary dwelling. The Brihadaranyaka Upanishad provides an interesting analogy to illustrate this point. It compares the body of the *jīvanmukta* to the discarded skin of a snake. The skin was a part of the snake before it was discarded. In fact, it was the snake itself. But once it discards the skin, even though the skin lies close to it, the snake is completely indifferent to it. It does not identify with it. The body of the *jīvanmukta* is like the skin that is shed by the snake. His identification with the body ended when his identification with the Self began. Even though his body is seen wandering around by others, he himself is completely unidentified with it. Only a person who is totally identified with the Self can live in such total awareness of the Self.

The Power of Practice

Is it possible for everyone to be liberated, or is liberation the monopoly of a few privileged individuals? Shankara says such questions persist when an eminent teacher and teaching are lacking. How can we expect to attain Self-Knowledge when we have no teacher who can give us that knowledge or when we make no effort of our own to study the scripture? Even if we succeed in acquiring some elementary knowledge of the Self, we make no serious effort to develop it into in-depth knowledge. We get distracted constantly by worldly matters. We cannot attain Self-Knowledge and experience the Self when our mind is constantly distracted. Even though Consciousness is our very nature and is in our immediate grasp, it will continue to evade us. We will continue to experience only multiplicity, not Oneness. Only rigorous disciplines, such as the practice of the six-virtues and the three-fold practice, will purify our minds and prepare us for Self-Knowledge.

Ways of the Jivanmukta

Shankara describes the state of a *jīvanmukta* beautifully in his Satasloki (100 verses) as follows: "When he moves about, a *jīvanmukta* feels like he is a wave rising in an ocean called Consciousness. When he is resting in one place, he feels like he is a luminous gemstone in the necklace called Consciousness. When he transacts with the world with his sense organs, he feels that he is witnessing himself in the effulgence of his own Self. When he goes to sleep, he feels like he is floating in an ocean of bliss called Consciousness. The *jīvanmukta* spends his life in this manner, continuously abiding in the Self and experiencing his Self as Pure Consciousness."

Shankara provides several beautiful analogies to describe the Self in relation to the world. He says that the Self is like the sweetness in a ball of jaggery and the fragrance in a lump of camphor. Every grain in the ball of jaggery is nothing but sweetness. Every grain in the lump of camphor is nothing but fragrance. Similarly, Self as Pure Consciousness permeates every object we perceive. It is inside and outside every object. There is no object that is separate from Consciousness. All objects appear and dissolve in Consciousness. Consciousness alone IS.

Such is the experience of *jIvanmukta*-s. They are not constrained by time, past, present, or future. Although they continue to live and mingle with us, we cannot fathom their ways. They live in total awareness of the Self while being alert to their tendencies, which are a residue of *prArabdha* karma. As aspirants of Self-Knowledge, we must be vigilant about our tendencies (*vAsanA-s*). If left unfettered, our tendencies can take over and wipe away our entire understanding of the Self. This is why the scripture cautions us against a wavering mind and instructs us to keep our minds pure and untainted. It even instructs us to take pure and uncontaminated (*sattvic*) food because pure food produces a healthy body and mind. When the body and mind are pure, *sattva* dominates over *rajas* and *tamas*. A mind that is pure and undisturbed by negative tendencies is capable of grasping the Self and abiding firmly as It.

Relentless Practice

Admittedly, it is a huge challenge to pursue the attribute-less Self (*nirguNa brahman*) for embodied people as Krishna says:

क्लेशोऽधिकतरस्तेषामव्यक्तासक्तचेतसाम्॥
अव्यक्ता हि गतिर्दुःखं देहवद्भिरवाप्यते॥

Bhagavad Gita 12.5

"For those whose minds are attached to the un-manifest, the path of realization is full of tribulations. Worship of the un-manifest is exceedingly difficult for embodied beings."

One may wonder if the *jIvanmukta,* who continues to have a body and has to attend to its needs from time to time, is also occasionally distracted from the Self. The body is not a distraction to the *jIvanmukta* because, as stated earlier, he does not identify with it or its needs. Shankara points out that theoretical Knowledge of the Self obtained in the first phase of *"shravaNa"* will only provide an intellectual understanding of the nature of the Self, but experiential Knowledge of the Self will help us grasp the Self "As It Is," without an iota of doubt. Such experiential Knowledge of the Self is achieved by the seeker in the second phase called *"manana."* Further effort made by the seeker to continuously abide in and as the Self is called *nididhyAsana.* Conceptualization of objects ends for the *jIvanmukta.* The world (*jagat*) and the individual (*jIva*) are not-Self (*anAtma*) because they perpetuate the feeling of separation. They dissolve and merge completely into a feeling of Oneness for the *jIvanmukta.* Dissolution of objects in this manner into the Self is called *pravilApana.* When all thoughts of separation dissolve and the feeling of Oneness prevails, the Self is experienced as Pure Consciousness. Such continuous experience of the Self is called abidance in the Self or single-minded devotion to the Self (*ananya bhakti*). This total absorption in the Self of the *jIvanmukta* is very different from the master-servant type of devotion that an individual has for a chosen deity with a specific form and attributes.

While some movements of the body are spontaneous, others like eating, sleeping, and bathing are intentional actions that we perform with the body. Even though the *jIvanmukta* is fully established in the unmoving and undifferentiated Self, he too has to occasionally move to perform bodily functions. However, the moment he completes the action, he once again resumes undifferentiated Consciousness. Externally, he might appear to be performing worldly actions, but internally, he remains unattached to them. This ability to be rooted in the Self while still transacting with the world is *nididhyAsana*. When all actions are performed with such total absorption in the Self, all transactions with worldly objects dissolve effortlessly into the Self.

The *jIvanmukta* continues the practice of *pravilApana* (dissolution of worldly objects) until his *prArabdha* karma is completely exhausted and his body is ready to die. The moment his body dies, both his practice and his transactions with the world come to an end. Since there is no residual karma remaining, he has no rebirth. Free of the body and mind, the *jIvanmukta* becomes a *videhamukta* and is freed from the cycle of birth and death.

The Teacher-Disciple Tradition

jIvanmukta-s function in two ways: they could be fully immersed in the Self or help other seekers in the world. Those who are fully immersed in the Self live in seclusion in a remote place like the Himalayas. Others continue to live in the middle of the society as the Divine Office-bearers. Some of them function as the Acharyas teaching Advaita. They move from place to place, teaching and uplifting individuals who yearn for Self-Knowledge. As soon as their karma is exhausted, these Acharyas discard their bodies and merge into Consciousness (as *videhamukta*-s). As a result of the training and inspiration they provided to seekers while alive, some of their students, in turn, mature into *jĪvanmukta*-s and continue to perpetuate the teacher-disciple tradition.

In this manner, the teacher-disciple tradition has continued for ages without a break and will continue to do so in the future. Inspired by *brahman*, *jĪvanmukta*-s uphold this tradition and are perceived as authorities on the subject. According to Shankara, Vyasa and other sages of the Upanishads were such inspired *jĪvanmukta*-s. Some of them acquired a new body after the death of the previous body, while others manifested a new body and entered it using their yogic powers. The moment their *prArabdha* or assigned karma completed, they discarded their bodies and attained complete liberation.

Just like the sages, the gods are also liberated beings who are specialized in particular domains. According to Chandogya Upanishad, the Sun will continue to operate as the eye of the world for a thousand *yuga*-s, after which it will cease all activity and dissolve blissfully into Consciousness.

अथ तत ऊर्ध्व उदेत्य नैवोदेता नास्तमेतैकल
एव मध्ये स्थाता तदेष श्लोकः ॥

Chandogya Upanishad 3.11.1

"Next, after giving to all living beings the fruits of their work, the Sun will be above such obligations. It will no longer rise nor set, and will stay by itself midway."

Only the wise recognize the greatness of *jIvanmukta*-s and seek their presence. They win the love of the *jIvanmukta* through humility and discipline, receive the teaching, and depart as awakened individuals. When a *jIvanmukta* facilitates such an awakening in an aspirant, he will be fulfilling his divine mission.

Videhamukti

Once their *prArabdha* is exhausted and they complete their mission on earth, *jIvanmukta*-s die and attain *videhamukti*. *videha* does not simply mean the death of the body. According to Shankara, *videha* means no more body after death (no rebirth). There is no need for a body when *prArabdha* karma is exhausted, and the results of past (*sancita*) and future (*AgAmi*) karma are burned in the fire of Self-Knowledge. When there is not even a trace of karma remaining, there is no *janma* (rebirth). Therefore, *videhamukti* is liberation from the cycle of birth and death.

Does the *jIvanmukta* die just like a common man, or is there anything special about his death?

Unlike the vital force (*prANa*) of the common man, the vital force of the *jIvanmukta* does not go anywhere. Only when karma is still remaining, *prANa* leaves the body and ascends upwards. When the gross body dies, *prANa* sits in the subtle body and ascends to other worlds depending on the person's karma. For instance, the *prANa* of a ritualist may go to the world of his forefathers, while the *prANa* of a worshiper may go to Satyaloka. The *prANa* of the *videhamukta* goes nowhere, since there is no longer any vehicle remaining for his *prANa* to travel in. Since his Self is Pure Consciousness, his karma and associated gross, subtle, and causal bodies are completely dissipated.

Like the waves that merge into the ocean, when the *videhamukta* dies, his life-force, body, and mind simply dissolve into Consciousness. Waves rise from the ocean, crash onto the shore, recede, and merge back into the ocean. Waves are nothing but water through and through. It is not possible to pinpoint the exact location where the waves dissolved into the ocean. Similar is the state of the *videhamukta*. In the epic Mahabharata, Sage Vyasa compares the manner in which a liberated being leaves the body to the manner in which a fish swims in the river and a bird flies in the air. Neither the fish nor the bird leaves any trace of their journey behind. Similarly, the *videhamukta* leaves no trace of his previous existence behind. When Sage Suka, the greatest amongst the *videhamukta-s,* died, it is said that his body merged completely into the five elements at lightning speed without a trace.

Death is an altogether different experience for those who spend all their life attached to worldly experiences and emotions. Since they live in ignorance with no knowledge of the Self, all their experiences in life are ephemeral. Since they spend their whole life believing that worldly objects and experiences are real, they die with the same tendencies (*samskAra-s*). Steeped in ignorance, they enter the great cosmic energy that keeps the wheel of *samsAra* turning. They continue in the cycle of birth and death.

Jivanmukti versus Videhamukti

Two beautiful examples illustrate the difference between a *jīvanmukta* and a *videhamukta*. The first example describes a wooden elephant installed in the middle of a city. Children gawk at the elephant in awe and fear, thinking it is real. Adults observe the elephant, knowing that it is not real. Fully aware of the substance that it is made of (wood), they recognize the shape of the elephant and clearly identify its legs, trunk, and other parts. With a firm grasp on the substance, they perceive the form that is superimposed on it. The *jīvanmukta* perceives his body-mind and the external world in a similar manner. He perceives names and forms without losing sight, even for a moment, of the substratum (Consciousness) on which they appear.

The state of the *videhamukta* is even more profound than the state of the *jīvanmukta*. The *videhamukta* is like a lump of salt dissolved in water. The salt dissolves completely in the water and loses its separate existence. Water that had once appeared as salt once again appears as water. Wherever you touch it, you only feel water. Like the lump of salt dissolved in water, names and forms dissolve completely into the Self, and Self alone remains.

The Nature of Videhamukti

Free of all limitations at the micro and macro level, the *videhamukta* has no place to go. He abides in the expansiveness of his own Self. As pure Existence and Awareness, his Self permeates and transcends everything.

एवमेवैष सम्प्रसादोऽस्माच्छरीरात्समुत्थाय परं ज्योतिरुपसम्पद्य
स्वेन रूपेणाभिनिष्पद्यते स उत्तमपुरुषः स तत्र पर्येति
जक्षत्क्रीडन्नममाणः स्त्रीभिर्वा यानैर्वा ज्ञातिभिर्वा नोपजनं
स्मरन्निदं शरीरं स यथा प्रयोग्य आचरणे युक्त
एवमेवायमस्मिञ्छरीरे प्राणो युक्तः ॥

Chandogya Upanishad 8.12.3 ॥

"The liberated *jīva* transcends the confines of his gross and subtle bodies and acquires a spiritual form luminescent with transcendental luster. This is his intrinsic, supramundane identity. He is a perfect being and resides in the spiritual world, relishing sublime activities and divine bliss at every moment."

We must be careful not to assume the words *transcend, enter,* and *attain* imply duality. There is no scope for duality in a liberated being. Sage Jaimini attributes omniscience and omnipotence to the liberated Self, but Sage Audulomi rejects this idea. Shankara accepts both viewpoints. From the relative viewpoint, Shankara says, Consciousness is all-pervasive and all-knowing. From the absolute viewpoint, the Self is Pure Consciousness devoid of all attributes. While embodied, Self appears differentiated due to the presence of the body-mind adjunct. After the death of the body-mind, Self resumes its original nature as undifferentiated Consciousness.

सर्वकर्मा सर्वकामः सर्वगन्धः सर्वरसः
सर्वमिदमभ्यात्तोऽवाक्यनादर एष म आत्मान्तर्हृदय
एतद्ब्रह्मैतमितः प्रेत्याभिसंभवितास्मीति यस्य स्यादद्धा न
विचिकित्सास्तीति ह स्माह शाण्डिल्यः ॥

Chandogya Upanishad 3.14.4

"He who is the sole creator, whose desires are the desires of all, whose odors are the odors of all, whose tastes are the tastes of all, who is everywhere, who has no sense organs, and who is free from desires – he is my Self and is in my heart. He is no other than Brahman. When I leave this body, I shall attain him. He who firmly believes this has no doubt in his mind. [He will surely attain Brahman.]"

The liberated Self can attain and experience anything by mere intention. There are many stories in the *purANa*-s that illustrate this. For instance, Sage Narada could roam the three worlds effortlessly, Sage Vishwamitra could create an alternate universe, and Sage Vyasa could temporarily give the blind King Dhritarashtra the vision to see his dead family members on the battlefield. If a *jIvanmukta* has such extraordinary powers, so does a *videhamukta*.

Since the *videhamukta* is Consciousness Itself, like Consciousness, he can play a dual role. He can transcend the world as well as be immanent in it. As Pure Consciousness, his Self transcends all objects and experiences only itself. This is a non-dual experience of the Self. As the manifestation of the Self in all objects, Self is immanent in every object and experiences every object and Itself! This is a dualistic experience generated by the Self of its own free will. Hence, the Self is capable of experiencing its own nature as non-dual Consciousness as well as experience the many. Only when the Self is capable of including everything in Itself, cause and effect included, will the Self be complete and perfect. Only when the Self is perfect, it is liberated.

भिद्यते हृदयग्रन्थिश्छिद्यन्ते सर्वसंशयाः।
क्षीयन्ते चास्य कर्माणि तस्मिन्दृष्टे परावरे॥

Mundaka Upanishad 2.2.8

"When he that is both high and low is seen, the knot of the heart is untied; all doubts are solved; and all his karma is consumed."

ॐ पूर्णमदः पूर्णमिदं पूर्णात् पूर्णमुदच्यते।
पूर्णस्य पूर्णमादाय पूर्णमेवावशिष्यते॥ ॐ शांतिः शांतिः शांतिः॥

Ishavasya Upanishad - shanti mantra

"That which is perfect will produce only that which is perfect."

Able to wield the power of *mAya* at his will, the *videhamukta* is in control of the creation and dissolution of the object world. He enjoys everything as the Self, while his Self remains as Pure Consciousness, untouched by experience.

सदेव सोम्येदमग्र आसीदेकमेवाद्वितीयम्।
तद्धैक आहुरसदेवेदमग्र आसीदेकमेवाद्वितीयं तस्मादसतः
सज्जायत॥

Chandogya Upanishad॥ 6.2.1॥

"Somya, before this world was manifest there was only existence, one without a second. On this subject, some maintain that before this world was manifest there was only non-existence, one without a second. Out of that non-existence, existence emerged."

Abidance in the Self is the natural state of the *jIvanmukta*. He enjoys all pleasures but remains unmoved and unattached to all experiences. Liberated from all bondage, he fulfills the ultimate goal of human birth. He entered the dwelling called the body, acquired the knowledge of the Self, and, with the power of Self-Knowledge, he became a *videhamukta*. His Self permeates the entire universe as Pure Consciousness. He becomes a *pUrNa puruSha*, a Perfect Being.

Conclusion

Freedom from suffering and the cycle of birth and death is liberation or *mukti*. *mukti* is of two types: *jIvanmukti* and *videhamukti*. The *jIvanmukta* continues to have a body and experiences the functions of the body due to *prArabdha* karma. But his body and mind appear to him as shadows, so they do not bother him. *jIvanmukta*-s are of two types: those who live in seclusion away from the society and those who live in the society, teaching others the Knowledge of the Self. Sages, such as Vyasa and Shankara, belong to this latter category. Divinely inspired, through their writings and teachings, these sages teach and uplift seekers. This wonderful teacher-disciple tradition continues to this day. Instead of letting the teaching remain as a theory locked up in the scripture, these sages make it their mission to spread the Knowledge of the Self widely and inspire seekers to experience the Self for themselves. When the body of the *jIvanmukta* dies, he becomes a *videhamukta*. Free of the cycle of birth and death, the *videhamukta* does not take another body. Along with the power of Self-Knowledge, he has in his control the power to manifest (*mAya*). Hence, he can remain as Pure Consciousness or manifest and dissolve the world at will. He can reveal or conceal his true nature at will. Capable of doing anything at will, he perceives everything as Self alone and experiences everything as Pure Consciousness. He attains perfection effortlessly, which is the ultimate goal of human life.

Afterword

We have now completed an in-depth study of the major principles of Shankara's Advaita philosophy. Since each chapter discussed each principle in detail, we have now attained a comprehensive view and holistic understanding of Shankara's Advaita teaching.

The first chapter established that the world we perceive as real is in fact unreal, and *brahman* (Consciousness) alone is real. If *brahman* alone is the Absolute Reality, why are we obsessed with names and forms? The second chapter explains that names and forms are a relative reality and are a means for us to grasp the Absolute Reality.

What is the process through which we can grasp the Absolute Reality? The third chapter answers this question by explaining that it is not through karma or ritualistic practices, but it is only through an understanding of our intrinsic nature (Self) that we can grasp the Absolute Reality.

What is the nature of the Self, and how can we experience It? The fourth chapter describes the process of first superimposing the not-Self (*anAtma*) on the substratum that is the Self (*Atma*) and then removing the superimposition to reveal the underlying reality that is the Self.

Why does this practice not produce the desired results uniformly for everyone? The fifth chapter explains that our past actions (karma) obstruct our current efforts, so we must purify our minds through the six-fold practice (*shama, dama,* etc.) and then practice *shravaNa, manana,* and *nididhyAsana* to experience our essential nature as Pure Consciousness.

The sixth chapter describes the result of such practices, the nature of *mukti* (liberation), and the life of a liberated being (*jIvanmukta*).

In a nutshell, introspection into our essential nature, contemplation on the nature of our Self, and a firm conviction that Self alone IS will free us from bondage and liberate us in this very life.

These profound insights are scattered across various works of Shankara. I collected and compiled them into this book. Although the book is based on Shankara's core teaching, I have taken some liberty in making minor modifications here and there to make the teaching relevant to the contemporary audience. I focused on capturing the intent of the author and the purport of the message he wishes to convey, rather than simply providing a literal translation of the original text. This might raise the eyebrows of some academicians and scholars. While it is important not to deviate from the original text, my request to such scholars is to delve deeper into the teaching and broaden their perspective and understanding.

Shankara himself is my role model. Although he advocated a teacher-disciple tradition, he himself was not satisfied with the explanations provided by his teacher. He contemplated deeply on the teaching, and his commentaries reflect the insights he attained through this contemplation. If we study Shankara's commentaries attentively, we will discover several new concepts and fresh expressions that we will not find in the earlier texts on Advaita. These insights may appear to be contradictory to the traditional teaching, but these are only apparent, not real contradictions. Shankara associates direct and indirect sources of Knowledge to *shruti* (Upanishads) and *smriti* respectively.

या निशा सर्वभूतानां तस्यां जागर्ति संयमी।
यस्यां जाग्रति भूतानि सा निशा पश्यतो मुनेः॥
Bhagavad Gita 2:69॥

"What all beings consider as day is the night of ignorance for the wise, and what all creatures see as night is the day for the introspective sage."

Shankara defined the word "*nishA*" in the above verse as *paramAtma*. He defines *Atma, yoga, prakriti*, and other terms in various ways throughout his texts. He also explained entire verses in this manner, customizing the definitions of terms to be relevant to the context in which they are being used.

Based on his own vast knowledge and experience, Shankara synthesized all opposing views in the scripture and presented them in a cohesive manner in his commentaries. He does not simply repeat what is in the scripture, but rather elucidates with elaborate reasoning and examples, bringing the concepts to life. Unless he rises beyond the obvious meaning (of the words of the scripture) to lofty levels of understanding, he will not be able to explain them in such lucid details. He asks us to also sharpen our intellect through contemplation and expand our understanding and insights. He says, Sage Badarayana advises us to not get stuck to the literal or traditional meaning of the scripture but to understand the spirit of the teaching and adapt it to the current context. As long as we do not deviate from the spirit of the scripture (truth) and do not compromise on the essential teaching, it does not matter exactly how we present it. Shankara never deviated from the spirit of the scripture. When he himself never did so, it is not possible for me, who followed in his tracks, to do so. Just as Shankara studied the original scriptures, contemplated their essential message, and captured the essence in his commentaries, I churned the vast ocean of Shankara's knowledge, extracted the cream of his teachings, and presented them to you in this book. There is no scope for any discord whatsoever; I can say so without any hesitation.

There is no need for either of us, the reader or the author, to aggrandize Shankara. Shankara is beyond ego. There is really nothing that we can offer him. We can only gratefully accept the Supreme Knowledge he has given us as his legacy. So vast and deep is his Knowledge that it makes every other knowledge (of objects) appear limited and shallow. The world is made of many countries. Each country is made up of people of different ethnicities. Each ethnicity has its own culture. Culture begins with a collection of beliefs or superstitions. Over time, after extensive analysis, a belief system develops into an organized science. Gradually, the science evolves into a philosophy that includes both the immanent and the transcendent. When philosophy matures, it culminates in a non-dual vision.

Hence, everything in this world begins in duality and ends in non-duality. This is true of all the popular religions of the world. Mysticism is a popular notion nowadays. Some believe that mystical experiences are the ultimate experiences of human life and strive to attain them. A mystical experience should be a non-dual experience, where the individual, the world, and the creator merge and become One. Shankara referred to the knowledge of the Upanishads as the secret or esoteric knowledge. He also called it *aparOkshAnubhUti*, the immediated and direct non-dual experience. All religions, including Islam, Judaism, Christianity, Jainism, and Buddhism, have this secret knowledge as their goal. As a religion evolves, new schools of thought develop and branch off from it. For instance, Zen evolved out of Buddhism, Christian mysticism evolved out of Christianity, and Tasavvuf (Sufism) evolved out of Islam. Although several dualistic philosophies, such as yoga and *sAnkhya,* evolved from the ancient culture of India, Advaita stands as the undisputed Supreme teaching. Every word of the Upanishads, great declarations such as *"brahman* is one without a second" and "All is truly brahman" reverberate with the feeling of Oneness.

We must be grateful to Shankara for the rich and profound knowledge he has left us as his legacy. Only a few people recognize and appreciate his greatness. Unlike Buddha and Christ, who are renowned across the world and have large followings, Shankara is less known to the world, even though his knowledge and wisdom surpassed that of these other teachers.

Shankara chastised many contemporary religions and their founders for propagating teachings that violate the spirit of Oneness that the Upanishads transmit. For instance, he chastised Buddhism for promoting two separate doctrines, *vijnAna vAda* (mind-based reality) and *sUnya vAda* (emptiness theory), which have no connection with each other. For something to be true, it must be constant (unchanging). How can Buddhism convey the truth when its doctrines are disconnected and not integrated? Such doctrines only confuse people and do not help people in their search for truth.

If we closely examine Shankara's perspective on Buddhism, we realize two things: 1) Buddha's character and behavior are exemplary, but right conduct is not the same as right experience. 2) Buddha's knowledge and experience did not transcend the intellect that undergoes constant change, from birth to death. By sharing his limited vision of reality (truth), Shankara says, Buddha misled the masses.

Shankara was only interested in revealing the truth about the Self and liberating individuals from ignorance. He was not interested in founding or organizing a religion and collecting masses as followers. He is a true Jagat-Guru, a World-Teacher, because he only cared to teach the Absolute Truth. Only someone like Shankara, who has experienced the Ultimate Reality, is capable of transmitting the truth about the Ultimate Reality. The experience of that Ultimate Reality is the Right Knowledge.

Referring to Mahavira, the Theerthankara (founder) of the Jain religion, Shankara said the following: "A Theerthankara has a huge responsibility because his followers consider him to be an authority on the subject, the source of Knowledge. Since every word he utters is perceived as truth, he must make sure that whatever he says can be verified in direct experience. If it cannot be verified, then his words are untrue and are of no value."

Regarding the *sAnkhya* tradition and its founder Kapila, Shankara says that Kapila is considered to be an accomplished sage but his accomplishments were a result of the vigorous practice of the various karmas described in the scripture (Vedas). How can Kapila, who is familiar with the scripture, perpetuate duality when the scripture itself is broadcasting non-duality? The scripture says that *prakriti* (nature) depends on Consciousness (*paramAtma*) for its existence, but Kapila insists that nature is independent and an entity in itself! Unfortunately, people worship Kapila as an authority even though his teaching violates the fundamental principles of the scripture. Shankara scolds such people for blindly following someone without any discrimination just because they have name and fame.

Shankara says those who blindly follow *dharma* (Mimamsa) without any introspection are worse than those who completely disregard the scripture. They have a wrong understanding of *Atma* and associate their ego with *Atma*. Every action they perform is with an attitude of "doer-ship." Such an attitude is an expression of the ego.

Logicians, according to Shankara, completely ignore what is readily present and argue about something that is only a figment of their imagination!

In this manner, Shankara chastised teachers and followers of different religions because they deviated from the truth. Feelings of separateness lead to division, not unification. As seekers of truth, we yearn for the One thing (Self) that is real and constant. We can grasp that One thing only when all feelings of separateness disappear, when the separate self (individual), world, and creator dissolve into the One.

Since all these religions only promoted duality, which changes constantly, Shankara says, they are far from truth. What is real does not undergo any change (*vikAra*). The unchanging (*nirvikAra*) Infinite Consciousness is the only Reality. It is the only source of Knowledge (*pramANa*). This is how Shankara established the authenticity of Advaita. No logic can dispute Advaita since it is the very nature of the Self. Hence, Shankara earned the exclusive title of "Jagat-Guru," the World-Teacher.

It is only to prevent them from spreading the wrong message that Shankara denounced other religions. He had no malice toward them. There can be no trace of duality, likes or dislikes, in a staunch Advaita practitioner like Shankara. Shankara was a self-critique. He often asked himself, "Isn't it better to teach those who yearn for Self-Knowledge, instead of debating with these others who don't? Arguments only lead to separateness," and answered himself, "Religions such as *sAnkhya* make false promises about liberation. Since such promises are made by influential people of the society, naïve individuals believe them. I need to reveal the shallowness of these religions and point people to the right path."

Shankara says that dualistic and nihilistic religions are based on differences, while Advaita is based on a non-difference (*ananya*). It considers the different religions as the different parts of the One entity – Consciousness. Even if followers of other religions ridicule them, Advaitins are not concerned because they are aware that these other religions are only a manifestation of the one reality, which is Pure Consciousness.

Hence, even when Shankara condemns other religions or their founders, he does so only to prevent them from misleading people. As a World-Teacher, he has a responsibility for making sure truth is not compromised in any way. With an unflinching resolve to ensure seekers of truth are pointed in the right direction, he traveled the length and breadth of the country, debating with opponents of Advaita, defeating them with his indisputable reasoning and logic, and establishing Advaita as the Truth. His unwavering and tireless efforts to correct all traditions that violate the non-dual spirit of the scripture and establish the Advaita teaching as the gold standard resulted in the wide dissemination of the Knowledge of the Self and the establishment of the four Advaita Ashrams in the four corners of India.

Those who do not understand or appreciate the greatness of Shankara criticize him in many ways. They accuse him of being attached to the Vedas, promoting a caste system, and encouraging rituals that involved animal sacrifices. They think he was just a narrow-minded Hindu who lacked a broad or lofty vision.

Such assumptions and accusations are meaningless and groundless. Shankara held the Vedas in the highest regard not because they are a collection of rituals and chants, but because they contained a treasure of wisdom in the form of Upanishads. Rituals and chants, according to him, are just an external expression of this internal wisdom. Behind the rituals and chants is the profound experience of the great seers of the past. Shankara says that rituals and chants are tools that prepare us for the higher Knowledge of the Self, but are not an end in themselves. If the scripture describes something that is not in our immediate experience, Shankara says, we do not have to blindly follow it. The scripture only describes that which is already present, and not something that is yet to be created. It can only describe objects that can be known (perceived), but *brahman* is not an object that can be known. Therefore, even the scripture does not directly and precisely describe *brahman*. It can only indirectly point us to it by describing its attributes, such as Infinite, Indivisible, Changeless, and so on. Once we understand the nature of *brahman* (Self) with the help of these attributes, we don't need the scripture anymore. The scripture has served its purpose and is of no further use to us. In this manner, while promoting Vedas as necessary, Shankara also clearly defined its boundaries. He discouraged blind attachment to the scripture and encouraged thorough analysis and understanding of its core value and limitations. There is no parallel in history to Shankara's scientific approach in interpreting the scripture.

We must remember that Shankara accepted both the Absolute and Relative realities. Although truth is only One (Consciousness), it appears as many based on people's perception. In accordance with the common perception of the relative world, Vedas provisionally describe various entities and actions (*karma kANda*), such as castes, rituals, and worship. None of these are real. They appear to be real and relevant only because of our ignorance (lack of Knowledge of the Self). When ignorance is removed with Self-Knowledge, all appearances lose their reality. As long as ignorance continues to exist, caste and other differences will continue to exist. The problem is not in the caste system itself, since the aim of the caste system is only to assign tasks to individuals based on the skills and capacities of individuals. The problem is in the ignorance of the individuals who blindly follow a system without any discrimination. We cannot be contemptuous of one thing (castes) and be attached to another thing (ignorance). As long as we identify with our body and mind and not with our essential nature, we will remain ignorant. As long as we remain ignorant, differences in the form of castes, rituals, and so on will continue to haunt us.

Rituals involving animal sacrifices are a result of both desire and ignorance. If we stop craving for things, we will no longer be interested in any rituals or sacrifices. Every action we perform is driven by a desire for a particular result. Since endless desires are a human tendency, the scripture prescribes actions (karma) to satisfy our desires. The scripture is like a lamp. Whatever action is performed in front of it, good or bad, the lamp is not affected. It simply stands as a witness. Similarly, the scripture offers everything. Depending on what we desire, we can find the corresponding information in the scripture. It does not force any actions on us if we have no desires!

Shankara did not teach anything new. He only taught what is in the scripture. The world is made of names and forms. But names and forms are mere appearances. They appear as real only due to misidentification with body and mind. Once Knowledge of the Self arises, the world disappears. What remains is the One Reality. Shankara unequivocally declared that Self alone is real. Standing as the Self, he melted all differences, rituals, castes, etc. into the Self. No teacher in the present or in the past has had the courage to accomplish what Shankara accomplished. While establishing the Self (Consciousness) as the Absolute Reality, he graciously accepted everything else as a relative reality. In this manner, he appeased both, the dualists who believed that the relative world is real and the Knowledge-seekers who believed that Self alone is Real.

Based on the above discussion, it is obvious that Shankara was not attached to a particular tradition or a caste. He described the Self as transcending all differences. He defined a Brahmin as a person who has the knowledge of *brahman*, and not as someone who belongs to a specific caste or class. He said that there is no need to perform any karma, and it is enough to have a burning desire for Self-Knowledge. He declared that Knowledge is not the exclusive privilege of a handful of gods or sages. Everyone, from an ant to the creator Brahma, has the right to Self-Knowledge. For a seeker who yearns only for Knowledge, castes, rituals, and chants are like the exotic palaces and cities that appear in a dream. For the one who has developed a universal vision of the Self, names and forms appear as superimpositions on Consciousness.

Shankara thus integrated everything into his panoramic vision. Such a universal vision is possible only for a *paripUrna* Advaiti, a perfect and complete non-dualist. Because of his universal vision, he is considered a Bhagavatpada, a divine incarnation. Since he strived for the spiritual upliftment of every individual on earth, he came to be known as the World-Teacher (Jagat-Guru). Anyone who yearns for truth, whatever country or race he or she belongs to, can freely tap into Shankara's ocean of wisdom. It is this ocean of wisdom that I channeled into these six chapters and made them available to all of you who seek the Supreme Knowledge. After reading this book, if you are able to firmly grasp the Self, contemplate and experience your Self as Pure Consciousness, I will feel that I have fulfilled my purpose in writing this book.

By the age of eight, Shankara mastered all the scriptures. By the age of twelve, he received initiation from an enlightened master. By the age of sixteen, he wrote elaborate commentaries on the scriptures. By the age of twenty, he traveled the length and breadth of the country, widely disseminated the Knowledge of the Self, received accolades from the rulers of the country, established four centers of Advaita in the four corners of the country, and nurtured several disciples into great teachers who later continued to spread his wisdom. By the age of thirty-two, he completed his mission on the earth and merged into *brahman*. He left behind a treasure of Knowledge to guide us in our search for Truth. We are blessed indeed to have such a teacher as Shankara. Shankara is the embodiment of everything Divine. He is Lord Ishwara Himself as well as the Sage Vyasa and the all-pervading Lord Vishnu.

Index

Made in the USA
Middletown, DE
08 November 2021